T0324541

THE ROAD TO RESILIENCE

THE
ROAD
TO
RESILIENCE

ARM YOURSELF FOR LIFE'S
CHALLENGES AND LEARN
HOW TO BOUNCE BACK

ADAM PRZYTULA

WILEY

First published in 2022 by John Wiley & Sons Australia, Ltd

42 McDougall St, Milton Qld 4064
Office also in Melbourne

© John Wiley & Sons Australia, Ltd 2022

The moral rights of the author have been asserted

ISBN: 978-0-730-39866-0

A catalogue record for this book is available from the National Library of Australia

All rights reserved. Except as permitted under the *Australian Copyright Act 1968* (for example, a fair dealing for the purposes of study, research, criticism or review), no part of this book may be reproduced, stored in a retrieval system, communicated or transmitted in any form or by any means without prior written permission. All inquiries should be made to the publisher at the address above.

Cover design by Wiley
Cover Images: Scribble: © enjoynz/Getty Images; Road: Wiley

Beyond Blue's Be You Mental Health Continuum © The Commonwealth of Australia represented by Department of Health

Internal figure credit: p34: © AKV/Shutterstock; p59: © leremy/iStock, © Leremy/Shutterstock; p82: © rassco/Shutterstock; p85: © rassco/Shutterstock; p139: © Vaclav Krivsky/Shutterstock, © rassco/Shutterstock

Disclaimer
The material in this publication is of the nature of general comment only, and does not represent professional advice. It is not intended to provide specific guidance for particular circumstances and it should not be relied on as the basis for any decision to take action or not take action on any matter which it covers. Readers should obtain professional advice where appropriate, before making any such decision. To the maximum extent permitted by law, the author and publisher disclaim all responsibility and liability to any person, arising directly or indirectly from any person taking or not taking action based on the information in this publication.

To Oma,
for the unconditional love,
compassion and care you showed me
and for inspiring me to start Armed For Life.

IMPORTANT NOTE TO READERS

This book has been written for educational and informational purposes only. It is not in any way intended to serve as a substitute for proper professional medical or psychological advice. Any views expressed in this book, or recommendations made, are the personal opinions of the author and should not replace medical or psychological guidance from a trained professional.

This book is also not intended to be used to diagnose or to treat any medical or health condition and the use of any information contained in this book is at the reader's sole discretion and is their sole responsibility.

Although every effort has been made to ensure accuracy and efficacy of the information in this book, the author specifically does not warrant the topicality, quality or correctness of the information provided and accepts no liability whatsoever in the event of its misuse, misinterpretation or any other act or occurrence that may be detrimental to any person.

Armed For Life: The Road to Resilience claims no sponsorship or affiliate relationship with any of the brands or professionals that may be cited or recommended in the work.

Contents

Acknowledgements

First, thank you Oma, for your unconditional love. I could write a whole book recognising all you have done for me and the fond memories I have (which I just may do one day). You continue to inspire me every day as much as you did while on this earth. I know you are in God's hands – and probably still looking out for me. I hope I honour you with everything I do for others.

Thank you to my wife Cherith for loving me the way I have always needed to be loved. For inspiring me with your faith, for being a part of God's plan to bring the healing I so needed, and for choosing to take this journey with me. I love you with all my heart!

Thank you to my son Cale for recognising I'm the boss (hahaha), but mostly for choosing to be you, regardless of what others say – because you are so special! I hope to help you to be a better version of me.

Dad, thank you for your support and encouragement with Armed For Life and for believing in me at times when I did not believe in myself. I have always known you love me – and always will. Thank you for instilling in me the work ethic I have (most of the time). You carry the spirit of Oma in your interaction with my boys and all your grandkids. She would be so proud!

Thank you Mum, for embedding in me the desire to always be clean and to live in a clean environment (which I am sure my wife is thankful for too). Seriously though, thank you for playing a role in shaping who I am, and mostly for the help you provided when it was needed most. I am so glad that Cale and Levi get to call you 'Oma' and experience a grandmother's love. Your involvement with our son Levi in particular has been an incredible blessing – especially those first four weeks. You just did *everything* – it was really special to have you with us. You were a rock for Cherith and me – and you continue to be. Thank you!

And to my brother Paul. Thank you for looking out for me in primary school (yes, I do remember those times). Just as you are often a negatron on your awesome podcast, *The Countdown: Movie and Television Reviews* (free plug – you're welcome!), you were often a negatron to me when I was a kid – that's okay though as I snuck into your room constantly and used your stuff (haha!). Our relationship and friendship have grown over the years and I really do appreciate the time we spend together. Thank you for paving the way for my absolute love of movies and for being there in the darkest times to help and support me. Proud to call you my bro!

Opa, thank you for the love and guidance you showed to Oma and to our family, and for making the hard journey with Oma from Germany and Poland to set up a life for us here in Perth, Western Australia.

To Phil Baker, the senior pastor at Riverview Church during my time on staff: your words made a difference to my path in life. Thank you.

To Sy Rogers (RIP): you were hugely influential to me – the kindness you showed me every time we met and my style of speaking have a lot to do with you.

Thank you Neil Chisholm, for your leadership and guidance.

Jarryd Smith at 2nd Chance Trust, thank you for your feedback on the manuscript and for writing the foreword to this book. Your friendship and fellowship have become very important in my own journey and that of Armed For Life.

Thank you to the friends who have stood by me and supported me when I needed it most – you know who you are. Ray, Steve and Jordan, thank you for caring for me in my darkest time. Your love and support have helped me to become who I am today!

And to Chris Burd: thank you for pushing me to write this book. It took me a while, but I got there.

I also want to acknowledge team members who have played a role in helping Armed For Life get to where it is now. Thank you to those who have been involved in the past, and thank you to those who currently play a large role:

- Mark Lloyd: I love what we do together bro – among my favourite school sessions to run. Thank you for supporting me personally and professionally. Love you bro!

- Taylor Cowper: you have enabled us to go to another level (and me to another country) in what we do with students. It means so much that I can trust you to run any topic. Thank you for supporting me no matter what and stepping up when I needed a go-to guy!

- Tam Hopper: you have been with me the longest, almost from the start. Not even moving to another country stopped you from continuing to support me. *You are amazing!* I honestly don't think we would be where we are if it wasn't for your voluntary work in the beginning. Thank you so much!

Thank you to Shannon Lancaster for collaborating with me to bring this book to life.

Thank you to my editor, Peter Ramshaw.

Finally, to you — whether you've listened to me speak or you've picked up this book and read it — thank you for supporting Armed For Life.

Foreword

Hey, I'm Jarryd and I'm the founder of 2nd Chance Trust and the author of two books, *180 Degrees: Had to Die. To Live* and *2 Billion Seconds.*

Two years ago, Adam told me he was writing a book about resilience and I knew it was going to be impactful. Now I've just finished reading the first draft and I'm not disappointed.

If you've ever felt alone or afraid, this book will definitely change that for you.

While I was sleeping on three crates and a cardboard box and given only three months to live because of my drug addiction, Adam was getting mercilessly bullied to the point he considered taking his own life.

Adam's story made me realise we all go through difficult struggles in life, but there is a way out and help is available. You have to speak up. Staying silent can kill you, but being honest and admitting where you're at is the most powerful thing you can choose to do.

This book gives you the tools to figure out what you should do when something happens in life to knock you down. They're simple principles which, if applied, can improve your life.

By sharing his own experiences, and with a good dose of practicality, Adam shows us how to take charge of our thoughts, how to become aware of our feelings and how to make good decisions that move us forward in life.

I won't lie, it's hard work committing to working on your pain and overcoming life's struggles. But it's worth it. My life is proof of that. If you're committed to changing your life, *this book is for you*!

Best wishes,
Jarryd Smith
Founder, 2nd Chance Trust
@2ndchancetrust

Introduction

Hey. I'm Adam Przytula and I run a social change enterprise called Armed For Life. You may have heard me (or one of my colleagues) speak at your school. We talk about some of the real issues you might be dealing with now or challenges you might be faced with in the coming years.

Why I wrote this book

I really struggled growing up. I was bullied every single day from Year 4 until the end of Year 12. At home, my parents were always fighting until I was in Year 8 when they got a divorce and Mum moved out.

I didn't know how to reach out and talk about what I was going through.

I thought I had to act tough and ignore the bullies. I tried to push down all my negative feelings. My life spiralled downwards until Year 10 when things got so bad, I almost ended my life.

My parents before their divorce

And I know I'm not alone.

Fast-forward 16 years to 2010. I was in my last semester of uni, studying to become a teacher. One day while working in a school, a student walked past me with his head cast downwards, biting his nails. I could feel the pain radiating from within him. I recognised myself: this kid was a younger *me*. He was trapped in pain and misery, just as I had been. At that moment, I knew I had to do something, and Armed For Life was born.

What I did next

I decided to start going into schools and talking to students openly and honestly about what I went through at school. As a student, I'd been too ashamed to speak out about what I was thinking and feeling, and I didn't know I should have spoken out. I wanted students who were in a similar position to know they weren't alone. There is help out there. They deserve to be listened to, supported and respected.

Home truths

It wasn't easy. I began talking to students about the real issues we all face in life, but I hadn't faced up to my own problems. I went through two messy divorces and a mental breakdown before I finally realised I needed to stop blaming other people for my problems and start taking responsibility for my own mental health and wellbeing.

I made a lot of mistakes and fell back into old, self-destructive behaviours countless times. But I worked hard to keep moving forward and I'll tell you about how I did it in this book.

How this book will help you

Some of the issues we face in life can be really challenging. Resilience is our ability to bounce back when times get tough. But this isn't something we're born with; it's a learnt skill. It's something we can get better at.

You might not have been through the same things that I've been through, but the tools in this book will arm you with the ability to face up to any challenge in life. No matter what your personal goal is (you might want to kill it in your exams or become an actor, start feeling good about yourself or make some new friends), the principles are the same.

Let me show you how.

Adam Przytula
Director, Armed For Life

chapter 1

Self-esteem

Congratulations on setting out on the road to resilience. In this chapter you will have the opportunity to learn about how you see yourself (your self-image), how much worth you think you have (your self-worth) and how you feel about who you are (your self-esteem). The most important thing I want to tell you is *you* are valuable. All of us have just as much worth as anyone else in the world. No-one ever has the right to make you feel as though you aren't worthy.

Having the internal belief that you are acceptable just the way you are is the foundation of healthy self-esteem. If you feel good about yourself, you'll be able to cope with whatever challenges life throws your way.

Be like Thor

Have you seen the movie *Avengers: Endgame*? It's the direct sequel to *Avengers: Infinity War* and the 22nd film in the Marvel series. You might love it, hate it or not care either way (I love *Avengers*), but stay with me for a second.

We're used to seeing Thor as a demigod. He's ripped, powerful and strong. Thor is a superhero. Thor knows he's valuable. That is, until *Avengers: Infinity War* when Thanos defeats the Avengers by using the Infinity Gauntlet to snap away half of all life in the universe. Thor loses his dad, his brother, his home and half of his people. He feels like he's failed. After all, what's the point of being strong if he's not strong enough to defeat Thanos? Enter what many dubbed online as 'Fat Thor'!

At the start of *Avengers: Endgame* we can see right away that Thor isn't feeling good about himself. He appears unwashed, unkempt and grossly overweight. Thor has turned to alcohol and gaming to try and cope with how low he's feeling. Thor's self-esteem is about as low as it can get, until the Avengers convince him to race back in time and retrieve the Infinity Stones before Thanos can get to them. Thor undergoes a huge internal battle against his depression and self-loathing. By letting go of his negative thoughts, Thor starts believing in himself again. I won't spoil the ending for you, but we see Thor's self-esteem start to spiral upwards.

Me

When I was a teenager, I hated myself. I thought I was worthless. My self-esteem was about as low as it could get.

Nowadays, I generally like myself. I feel good about who I am. I think I have relatively healthy self-esteem. The change is remarkable.

You

Like me and Thor, you can do stuff to change your self-esteem, but first you need to identify where you are at.

Let's see where exactly it is that you're at by doing this quiz together.

Try this

Personal self-esteem quiz

First of all, we need to look at where your self-esteem is currently sitting. Read through the following statements and tick those you agree with. If you're currently reading a hardcopy version of this book, I encourage you to use a pencil so that you can erase your answers and complete the quiz again once you've finished reading the book.

- ☐ **I desperately want to change the way I look.**
- ☐ **I find it difficult to accept who I am.**
- ☐ **I have really high standards for myself and for others (I am a perfectionist).**
- ☐ **I feel uncomfortable around successful people.**
- ☐ **I have high levels of anxiety and fear.**
- ☐ **I never try new things—I might make a mistake.**
- ☐ **I focus on my mistakes and minimise what I achieve.**
- ☐ **I feel down all the time.**
- ☐ **I frequently think negative thoughts about myself.**
- ☐ **I feel worthless.**

RESULTS

If you ticked one or more of the statements above, you may be experiencing low self-esteem. If you ticked even one statement, you need this book.

If you didn't tick any of these statements, it means your self-esteem is probably pretty healthy at the moment. That's great, but remember that self-esteem isn't something that stays the same; it can change depending on how you're thinking, or what challenges or problems or victories you're facing in life.

The self-esteem spiral

When something happens to us (it doesn't have to be as major as failing to save the universe – we might get bullied or go through a challenge of some other sort), we either think positively about the situation, or we think negatively.

When we think positively about a situation, we are more likely to make positive choices about how to act or behave. When our actions reflect our positive thoughts, we feel good about ourselves. We feel valuable. This means that our self-esteem spirals upwards.

If we experience negative thoughts, we tend to act on these thoughts by behaving in ways that aren't good for us or beneficial for those around us. It makes us feel bad about ourselves. We may start feeling like we aren't worthy or valuable. Our self-esteem spirals downwards.

Thinking negatively

Affects our behaviours

Affects how we feel about ourselves (self-esteem)

Which causes us to think more negatively

My story

As a kid, I loved running. Standing on the track, feeling the air fill my lungs and the sun against my skin felt good. Taking off, feeling my muscles engage and my heart beat as my feet pounded the grass felt really good. Passing the finish line first, having everyone cheer me on and winning the race felt really, really, *really* good. From Years 1 to 3, I was 'Champion Boy' and the best runner in my class. I loved being picked to go last in the relay because everyone knows the fastest kid goes last.

Being sporty meant I was automatically popular at school. It also made me feel like I was *valuable*, liked and accepted.

Things were the opposite at home. Although I knew my parents loved me, the constant yelling and arguing between them was scary and stressful. My big brother Paul was four years older than me, and it felt like I hardly knew him. It doesn't seem like much now that we are older, but four years is a lot when you're a kid.

This photo of me with my brother Paul was taken when he was 10 and I was 6.

Don't get me wrong, there were brief periods when it felt like we were just a normal family (like on Sunday afternoons when we'd sit around together watching Disney movies and eating McDonald's). However, most of the time I felt pretty lonely at home. It didn't feel like I belonged and I didn't feel valuable. So I started looking outwards for a sense of self-esteem.

At first, running provided me with the sense of value that I was desperately seeking. Then, in Year 4, I had to start taking steroids to treat eczema on my feet (yep, I was on the 'roids at the tender age of nine). Pretty rapidly I stacked on the KGs. The

(continued)

steroids made me supersized. I'd stand on the track at school, acutely aware of my belly beneath the tightly stretched fabric of my green faction t-shirt (go green!). It felt like everyone was laughing at me. As I took off, I felt my belly jiggle and I'd see other kids overtake me. Passing the finish line, puffing, I'd feel ashamed. I lost the title of Champion Boy. I started finishing second ... third ... then fourth. By Year 7 I'd dropped to the B Division in sports. I wasn't any good at running anymore.

So, I just gave up.

My long, painful downward spiral

In *Star Wars* (I love *Star Wars*), Master Yoda explains, 'Fear leads to anger; anger leads to hate; and hate leads to suffering'. This was me. From Year 4 until Year 7 I became more and more afraid of losing my sporting ability because it was the only thing that made me feel good about myself. In Year 4, I started getting bullied. By the time I reached Year 7, the kids who were supposed to be my friends beat me up instead, leaving my confidence in tatters. (I'll share this story with you later in the book.)

I went into Year 8 (the first year of high school in Western Australia at the time) with my self-esteem having spiralled to an all-time low. I had completely stopped trying at school. I hated myself, and it was really painful.

No-one ever told me that it was okay to feel things. I didn't know that our emotions are a really important part of who we are. I don't blame my parents because they didn't know any differently and they acted in ways that tended to be 'normal' for their generation: ignoring negative feelings or reacting with anger. I grew up thinking this was normal. I thought I had to push down my anger and push away my negative feelings and pretend they weren't there. This had a huge impact on my self-esteem.

How do you improve your self-esteem?

Just remember, if you're struggling with low self-esteem, it's not your fault. It's not because you are a 'bad person'. It's not because you were born with the self-esteem 'part' of you missing.

If you have low self-esteem, it means that, right at this moment in time, you aren't feeling too crash hot about yourself. And that's okay! Self-esteem is something we can work on and improve.

As humans, I believe we are born with two ingrained psychological needs: we need to feel loved, and we need to feel like we belong.

If we don't get these needs met (at home and at school) when we're growing up, it can be really hard to develop healthy self-esteem. When I was a kid, I didn't understand why I felt angry all the time. Although I knew Mum and Dad loved me, it didn't *feel* like I was part of a loving family because of all the fighting going on. When I was getting bullied at school, I thought it was because there was something wrong with me. I thought I was an outcast, a freak. I didn't feel loved, or like I belonged, at home or at school. Now I realise that I wasn't unique. Lots of other students go through similar things to what I went through, and far worse. Resilience is about being able to bounce back from the problems we face, and if we don't feel valuable, it's impossible to overcome life's challenges.

So, how do we start working on improving our self-esteem? Here are some tools you can use to help build your self-esteem:

- Change the way you think.
- Be self-aware.
- Choose your friends and relationships wisely.
- Be grateful.
- Talk to someone.
- Change your lifestyle.

Let's take a look at each of these tools in more detail.

Change the way you think

The human mind does one heck of a lot of thinking. Some psychologists suggest that the average human brain has up to 60 000 thoughts a day! But hang on – 95 per cent or so of these thoughts are actually the same ones we had the day before. What's more, around 85 per cent are *negative* thoughts. These thoughts seem to pop up out of the blue. But why do we have them?

If you're interested in psychology, or if you've studied it at school, you might have heard of a famous psychiatrist called Dr Aaron Beck. He's known as the father of cognitive behavioural therapy (CBT). In the 1960s, Dr Beck spent a lot of time working with patients who were experiencing symptoms of depression. Dr Beck noticed that his patients were experiencing repetitive thoughts such as:

'I'm not good enough'

'I always fail'

'I'm such an idiot'.

Dr Beck called these 'Automatic Negative Thoughts'. He became convinced that Automatic Negative Thoughts affected his patients' happiness and confidence, and contributed to their depression.

WHAT ARE AUTOMATIC NEGATIVE THOUGHTS (ANTS)?

Automatic Negative Thoughts are also known as 'ANTs'. The thing is, we *all* have ANTs. It's normal. Our brains are wired to think negatively because ANTs exist to keep us safe. How so? In prehistoric times, our ancestors relied on negative thoughts for their survival. Random thoughts helped keep them alive. For example:

'Don't eat that – it might be poisonous!'

'What's that noise? I'm being hunted!'

However, ANTs aren't nearly as useful for those of us who are living a fairly cosy existence in the twenty-first century. We might be trying to shoot a goal in basketball when a thought pops up: *Don't shoot — you'll miss!* or *What's that whispering? My teammates are laughing at me.* These ANTs don't help us to survive. In fact, they often prime us for failure.

The tricky thing about ANTs is that they often come from deep beliefs we have about life. Often, ANTs seem so true that we don't notice when we're having one, and we don't stop to question it. Instead, we just start feeling bad about ourselves without really knowing why. So how do we overcome ANTs?

HOW TO MASTER YOUR THOUGHTS

Your brain is a muscle. Just like any other muscle in your body, it needs exercise. Instead of running, jumping or dancing for exercise, your brain gets a workout by *thinking.* Each time you have a thought, a different neural pathway in your brain is exercised. The more 'reps' you do of this thought, the stronger the neural pathway becomes. If you do a hundred bicep curls every day, you'll notice your biceps getting bigger (and at first, really sore). Similarly, if you think, 'I'm stupid' one hundred times every day, the neural pathway associated with that thought grows stronger. The thought becomes more ingrained, more believable and more automatic.

Instead of letting ANTs happen, you can choose to be aware of your thoughts by using your feelings as a cue. How?

First, if you start to feel down, try to identify the thought that caused this.

Second, challenge the thought. Ask yourself, 'Is this thought true?' Just because your mind is telling you something, it doesn't automatically make it fact.

My story

A few years ago, I was playing in a really good basketball team. It was halfway through the season and we'd won every match. We'd also won the previous season. One night, I was driving home when an ANT popped up in my mind: *We scored 85 points tonight, but I only scored four. I must be 'That Guy' (the guy no-one wants to pass the ball to because he'll mess up and ruin the game).* The thought seemed to come out of nowhere, but I challenged it: *You're having an ANT. Just because you're thinking something, it doesn't make it true.*

After our next game, I approached a guy on our team who was an incredible player.

'I'm thinking about stepping off the team,' I confessed.

'Nah, man, don't do that,' he said. 'We need you. Every time you step off the court our lead decreases because your rebounding and your defence are so strong.'

During the next match, I took more notice of how I contributed to the team, and I saw he was right. My job wasn't to take possession and score. I was a defender. That's right: I wasn't MJ (Michael Jordan), I was Dennis Rodman. Basketball teams need both types of players.

If I hadn't called myself out though, I would have gone into the next game acting like 'That Guy'. I would have been thinking, *No-one wants to pass me the ball.* This ANT would have affected my confidence and my game. Then my teammates *really* might not want to pass me the ball, and I'd risk *really* becoming 'That Guy'. But I became aware of the ANT and I squashed it. By fact-checking with another player and weighing up the evidence, I realised what I'd assumed wasn't true. I replaced my ANT with a positive thought—*I'm a good defender*—and it boosted my self-esteem.

Two weeks later I severed my ACL (a ligament in my knee). It took me 12 months to get back on the court. Two weeks after I did my ACL, my basketball team lost their first match in two years. This reinforced to me that I wasn't the guy no-one wanted to pass the ball to. My role on the team wasn't to score points, but that didn't mean I wasn't a valuable team member. From that point on, I had the conviction — and the repeated positive thought — that my team needed me to be able to function well.

Here is a photo of me excited about my first basketball match after tearing my ACL.

When I returned to basketball after recovering from my injury, I had to join a new team because my old team had fallen apart. We were winning three seasons in, and I started playing attack instead of defence. I was regularly scoring 20 to 25 points each game. I put this down to having improved my thinking around basketball, and actively working on raising my self-esteem.

You too can ward off those ANTs by choosing to be aware of your thoughts and identifying whether or not they're true.

Try this

Nip your ANTs in the bud

For the rest of today and tomorrow, I want you to try and catch any Automatic Negative Thoughts (ANTs) you experience. Pay attention to how you're feeling, and if you start to feel down or discouraged out of nowhere, identify the ANT causing it.

If you're not sure whether your ANT is a true fact or not, check with someone. Don't ask your mum if you're beautiful/good looking though because, of course, she's going to say yes (unless you have a very real and honest relationship with her). Ask a trusted, but neutral, adult: a teacher, an adult you look up to and see as a mentor. This might be your auntie/uncle or a next-door neighbour.

Don't jump on *ASKfm* or any of your socials. Just don't.

Be self-aware

Self-awareness is about understanding your needs, desires, failings, habits and what makes you tick. If you take the opportunity to learn about yourself, it will be easier to deal with life's challenges.

A big part of self-awareness is understanding your emotions. As I mentioned before, it's okay to *feel*. Your emotions are valid. You will have feelings about yourself that are unpleasant. Sometimes these feelings stem from ANTs. Sometimes they occur because of something someone says about you, or something that happens to you.

It's normal to want to push down or ignore nasty feelings. Have you ever had a rush of anger or despair so strong that it feels like you can't cope? This happens because negative feelings build up inside us like a pressure chamber until, eventually, we can't contain them anymore and we either explode or experience a meltdown.

Being self-aware means that instead of trying to hide your feelings, or push them away, you choose to pay attention to the emotion and what it's trying to tell you.

My story

When I was a teenager, I didn't know what self-awareness was. By Year 8, my self-esteem had spiralled downwards. I blamed my problems on other people: my parents for splitting up; most of the kids at school for bullying me. My ANTs were getting worse. *Everyone hates me,* I thought. *I don't have any friends. I'm ugly and I'm fat.* The ANTs were making me feel depressed and anxious. Things were getting worse by the day.

During this time, there was one person in my life who I knew truly cared about me: my grandmother, whom I called 'Oma' because she was German. Oma and my grandfather (Opa) had fled Europe after World War II because he was Polish and their relationship was frowned upon at the time, if not yet downright *verboten*. Oma was a nurse, both during the war and when she and Opa moved to Australia. Oma was known for her caring nature. All of the kids on Oma's street used to visit Oma with scraped knees, insect bites and various other injuries. As he became older, Opa developed Parkinson's disease and Oma became his full-time carer. I don't have a lot of memories of Opa as he tended to keep to himself, but Oma had a huge influence on my life.

Here is a photo of Oma as a young woman living in Germany.

(continued)

When Mum and Dad split up, Mum moved out and Dad started working really long hours. He would be gone from 6 o'clock in the morning until at least 7 o'clock in the evening. Sometimes he wouldn't come home until close to midnight. Not long after, my brother moved out. I was on my own a lot. Time felt like a gaping hole and the hours seemed to stretch endlessly before me. I actually missed the noise of Mum and Dad yelling and arguing with each other.

Every morning, Oma would drive to my house to make sure that I got out of bed, ate breakfast and went to school. This was no easy feat for Oma. I'd wake up each day filled with a sense of dread. I knew I was going to get bullied, but I didn't know when it was going to happen. When I arrived home from school, Oma was always there, cleaning and cooking. Oma's presence was comforting. I soaked up the unconditional love and attention she offered me. At the same time, I dreaded the moment she'd need to leave to go and take care of Opa. Each evening, 6 o'clock rolled around and Oma's car would drive away. An overwhelming sense of despair would surge within me. The hours stretched endlessly before me. There was no relief in sight.

At the time, I didn't understand what was happening to me. I knew I was feeling depressed and anxious, but I tried to push these feelings down and ignore them. The only thing that got me through each day was the sense of comfort and unconditional love that Oma gave me. But my emotional state continued to plummet. I hated myself. My grades began to suffer. I started turning to behaviours that I thought were helping, but that were actually only making things worse.

COPING MECHANISMS

When we're feeling stressed, or experiencing negative feelings, it's normal to turn to the things that help us cope. These are known as 'coping mechanisms'. Not all coping mechanisms are created equal. For example, going for a run might help someone cope with feelings of stress or anxiety. Another person might turn to alcohol to help them cope with their emotions. A coping mechanism may be considered healthy or unhealthy. A 'healthy' behaviour might be considered 'unhealthy' in large quantities, and vice versa. We'll look at this further in chapter 4.

It's important to be aware of what your coping mechanisms are. They act as important red flags for ANTs and negative feelings. If you find yourself *needing* to use your coping mechanism to 'feel better', then it's important to question *why*.

My story

During my teenage years, I turned to binge eating. I wasn't self-aware. I didn't realise I was binging on lollies, chips and chocolate to try and numb the emotional pain I was experiencing. I just knew that eating junk food made me feel better. As a young kid, I'd always raided Oma's pantry for a couple of treats after school. But, by the time I reached high school, one or two chocolate bars weren't enough. Spending so much time alone at home, I smashed bags of the stuff, eating beyond the point of comfort until I felt physically sick.

I also developed a screen addiction. It started with movies and gaming, but soon the 'fix' I was getting from them wasn't enough. I gravitated towards pornography. What started out as a 'feel-good' coping mechanism descended into mental addiction.

As my junk food, screen and pornography addictions worsened, I began to feel more depressed and anxious. I started staying up all night because I didn't want to go to bed and have to face my thoughts. Inevitably, sleep deprivation made all of my problems worse. It was a revolving door of self-abuse.

WHAT SHOULD I HAVE DONE DIFFERENTLY?

By the age of 11, I was struggling but trying to put on a brave face.

I depended on unhealthy behaviours (binge eating and staying up all night to watch TV, game and watch pornography) to help me feel better. This is the opposite of being self-aware.

I should have paid attention to my ANTs and challenged them. Instead, I ignored how low I was feeling. The result? My self-esteem hit rock bottom.

HOW TO BE SELF-AWARE

Self-awareness is about paying attention to your *self* and being *aware* of your thoughts:

- Pay attention to your thoughts.
- Challenge ANTs.
- Pay attention to your feelings.
- If you're feeling a certain way, ask *why*.
- Identify your coping mechanisms: these behaviours are red flags.

Practising the following steps will help you overcome relying on coping mechanisms.

Try this

Be aware of your coping mechanisms

Answer these questions in your head and think about your answers intently.

1. What is one of your coping mechanisms?

2. When was the last time you used your coping mechanism?

3. How were you feeling before you used it? (It might be one dominant feeling, such as fear or anger. Or, it might be a mixture of feelings, such as feeling excited and nervous.)

4. What triggered you to have these feelings?

5. What ANT did you experience?

6. Challenge this ANT. Is it true?

Practise this exercise as often as you can. Next time you find yourself turning towards a coping mechanism, follow the steps above and see if you can identify the thoughts and feelings that caused you to need it. The more often you try to be self-aware, the easier it becomes.

Choose your friends and relationships wisely

There's whole chapters about friendships and relationships later in this book (see chapters 7 and 10) because healthy relationships (including friendships) are essential for healthy self-esteem.

HEALTHY FRIENDSHIPS

In a nutshell, if we have healthy friendships, we feel secure. We feel confident. We feel accepted. Regardless of whether we screw up and make a mistake.

Remember, as human beings we have two psychological needs:

- We need to feel loved.
- We need to feel like we belong.

Real, healthy friendships fulfil this need.

The quality of friendships is more important than the quantity.

Banter can be fun. It helps us to connect with each other, but we should come away from it feeling good about ourselves. If our friends tear us to shreds and don't support us, the constant negativity will start to bring us down.

HEALTHY RELATIONSHIPS

Relationships have a huge effect on our self-esteem. Why?

Because they're risky. Connecting on a deep level is the most rewarding thing we'll ever go through. It can also be the most painful.

Your relationship should make you feel supported, valued and accepted.

Arguing is normal. It forms a part of every relationship. However, there's a difference between healthy conflict and destructive conflict.

Be grateful

Being grateful means focusing on the good stuff in your life and feeling thankful instead of focusing on the negative things.

If you practise gratitude, it boosts your self-esteem. How?

Replacing ANTs with positive thinking makes you feel good. This makes you act in ways that make you feel even better. (Remember the self-esteem spiral.)

HOW TO PRACTISE GRATITUDE

Practising gratitude is an extension of being self-aware. It involves using your senses (see, hear, taste, feel, smell) to be mindful. That is, to be *in the moment.*

Being grateful means practising self-awareness: paying attention to the thoughts you are having. Taking notice of how you are feeling. Replacing ANTs with positive thinking.

Try this
How are you thinking and feeling right now?

Take a moment to tune into your senses:

- What can you see?

- What can you hear?

- What can you taste?

- What can you smell?

- What can you feel?

Reflect on these sensations to answer the following questions:

1. What are you thinking about?

2. If your thoughts are ANTs, can you reframe them into positive thoughts?

(continued)

3. How do your positive thoughts make you feel?

4. Based on this thought and these feelings, what do you have to be grateful for?

Here's an example of what I'm thinking and how I'm feeling right now.

Me

Right now, I can see my older son, Cale, in the rear-view mirror, and I hear him laughing at me as I describe this to you. I can feel the sun beaming through the window and it's warm against my skin. I can taste syrupy sugar because we stopped off for a coke and I can smell a mixture of sweat, air-con and fresh fruit because our grocery shopping is on the back seat.

I'm thinking that seeing Cale reminds me that he's the one really good thing to come out of my previous marriage. Cale is really funny, and we've had a great weekend together. The weather has been beautiful, and at this time of the year, we can buy strawberries together from 'our spot'. I swear they are the best strawberries in WA.

I'm feeling loved, relaxed and happy. I'm in a good mood.

I'm grateful I have Cale.

I'm grateful it's spring.

I'm grateful Cale and I got to spend the weekend together.

I'm grateful strawberries are for sale.

WHY PRACTISING GRATITUDE BOOSTS OUR SELF-ESTEEM

Choosing to feel grateful for what we have, instead of dwelling on what we don't have, has the effect of rewiring our brain. Remember I mentioned earlier about how when we practise a thought over and over, the neural connection becomes stronger? When we spend time practising gratitude, thinking positively becomes automatic. We behave in a positive way that causes us to feel good about ourselves. It's a great way to boost our self-esteem, and it has the added effect of attracting others to us.

Talk to someone

Gender is different now from how it was when I was growing up. It's a subject that can be polarising. What we are certain of, however, is that some things are still seen as 'masculine' or 'feminine'.

I used to think that talking to a counsellor was soft or weak. I thought that 'talking to someone' was touchy-feely, and that it was okay for girls to talk about their problems, but not for guys. I couldn't have been more wrong.

There is hard science behind why we need to reach out and talk about our problems.

When we speak aloud, it allows our brain to organise and make sense of the thousands of thoughts running through our minds. I personally feel everyone in the world should talk to a counsellor or psychologist at some point in their lives. Why?

TALKING TO SOMEONE CAN IMPROVE YOUR SELF-ESTEEM

This isn't a book about neuroscience and I'm not a scientist. However, I do know that talking to someone who specialises in listening to your problems will physically change your brain through the activation and firing of neurotransmitters. You can literally change:

- how you think
- how you feel *physically*
- how you feel *emotionally*

- how you look

- how you see yourself.

It might take time to find the right person to confide in: someone you connect with and someone you trust. Don't give up if it doesn't work out the first time, or even the tenth time. Keep trying. I spoke to three different counsellors before I found one who worked for me.

Change your lifestyle

Did you know that eating junk food affects your hormones and brain chemistry?

I didn't know this when I was in high school. I had no idea about:

- serotonin (the 'happy' brain chemical)

- dopamine (the 'feel good' brain chemical)

- cortisol (the 'stress' hormone).

I didn't realise binging on sugar, not working out, not getting enough sleep and watching pornography didn't just affect my physical health, it affected my mental health too.

You can read more about serotonin, dopamine and cortisol in chapter 4.

WHY CHOOSING A HEALTHY LIFESTYLE IMPROVES YOUR SELF-ESTEEM

When you decide it's important to be healthy, you choose to value and respect your mind and your body. Your mind will repay you by thinking clearly. Your body will thank you by performing at its best. You'll feel really good.

Living a healthy lifestyle doesn't mean you need to have a perfect diet, exercise every day and sleep eight hours every night. I'm all about the 80/20 rule. I eat healthily 80 per cent of the time so I can eat whatever I like 20 per cent of the time.

WHY YOU NEED A HEALTHY SELF-ESTEEM

Having a healthy self-esteem is vital.

It means we can deal with any of life's challenges with ease.

We all experience problems in life – it's inevitable. But having the skills to deal with problems as they come up makes life easier, more enjoyable and more fulfilling.

You've got this!

Answer these questions to revise what you've learned about self-esteem.

1. Can you think of a movie, book or TV series where a character starts out with low self-esteem but by the end of the movie/show has developed high self-esteem?

   _____

2. What did the character in question 1 do to improve how they felt about themselves?

   _____

3. Do you think it's possible you might see yourself differently from how others see you?

   ☐ Yes ☐ No

   If you answered yes, in what way do you think you might see yourself differently from how others see you?

   _____

   _____

4. What Automatic Negative Thought (ANT) do you experience often?

   For example, I used to always think, *I'm ugly because I have narrow eyes and a big forehead.*

   Write down your ANT:

   _____

   _____

5. Can you rephrase your ANT in question 4 into a positive thought?

   For example, I've rephrased my thought to: *I have my Opa's eyes and forehead. My Opa was Polish and survived the war. I'm really proud to be his grandson.*

   Write down your positive thought:

   _____

   _____

6. Do you consider yourself to be self-aware ('tuned in' to what you're thinking and how you're feeling)?

   ☐ Yes ☐ No

7. A coping mechanism is a behaviour or action you tend to turn to during times of stress. What are some of the coping mechanisms you usually turn to?

   _____

   _____

8. Think about your friendships and relationships.

   a. Is there someone in your life who makes you feel good when you're around them?

      ☐ Yes ☐ No

      What is it about this person that makes you feel good?

      _____

      _____

   b. On the flipside, is there someone in your life who makes you feel negative about yourself?

      ☐ Yes ☐ No

Why do you think this is?

_____

_____

9. What are five things you are grateful for right now?

_____

_____

_____

_____

_____

10. Identify someone you can talk to about how you are feeling
or the things you are going through. You can either write
down their name, or write the role they play (e.g. teacher,
family member, school counsellor).

Note: This person should be an adult. They should also be
objective, meaning they will be honest with you and tell you
things as they really are.

_____

_____

chapter 2

Resilience

Why do we talk about resilience? It's been a buzz word for quite a few years and soon another cool buzz word is sure to take its place (in fact, the word might have already changed – to 'grit'), but it's the meaning of the word that's important.

What is resilience?

One thing can be guaranteed in life – you will have problems. Resilience is all about being able to bounce back when those problems hit.

My story

If you've heard me talk before, chances are you've heard about the time in Year 10 when my wallet got 'stolen' at school and I ended up facing off with a drug dealer. The story goes like this.

'What does it look like?' asks Mr Brown, my physical education teacher.

'It's black,' I answer, and Mr Brown rolls his eyes at me.

'Black? Of course it's black, Adam. Most wallets are black. Does it have any money in it? Any cards?'

(continued)

I nod. 'Yeah, there's a 20-dollar note. My bank card. And a video store card.'

Mr Brown nods. 'Okay, I'll sort it out. Go and get changed.'

'Thanks.' I turn around and head back into the locker room. Voices bounce off concrete pillars as kids yell at each other, pushing, shoving and messing around. The pungent scent of sweat and urine mixed with Lynx covers the air like a thick blanket. There are gym towels, dirty socks and sweaty clothes strewn over every surface. In the far corner sits my bag, untouched since I stormed off a few minutes earlier. I feel a punch hit the middle of my back, throwing me forwards, and a laugh as I scramble to catch my balance.

'Get out the way, Bra-zoola!' (Bra-zoola was a nickname given to me in high school — I explain how it came about in chapter 3.)

As I turn around, an enormous red face looms towards me. Sweat quivers from the tip of its nose and drips from its chin. I turn back and walk over to my bag. As I strip off my shirt, Mr Brown storms back into the locker room.

'Boys, listen up,' he roars, and the room goes silent. Mr Brown rarely comes into the change rooms. His lips are pursed, forehead drawn. Usually relaxed, his stern expression doesn't suit him.

'What's up Browno?' asks the enormous red face and Mr Brown shoots him a dark look.

'Adam's wallet has been taken from his bag. I would like for whoever took the wallet to own up immediately,' he says, with a voice lowered and serious. Everyone looks at me, and I feel the heat rush to my cheeks as I stand there, my gut hanging over my belt, my slightly less than 'attractive' body out on display. The group of students look at each other shrugging.

'No idea, Mr Brown.'

'Wasn't me.'

'I dunno where his wallet is,' they say.

Mr Brown turns his gaze to each and every student, in turn. 'I'm giving one more chance to the person who took Adam's wallet to own up,' he warns. 'Otherwise, there will be a bag search.'

Bodies tense all around. No-one wants to have their bag rifled through by a teacher. I can feel the gaze of 30 sets of eyes firing their hatred in my direction. Some of the students begin to look disinterested.

'Can we go now?' A student looks at his watch and sighs.

'Finish getting changed,' Mr Brown orders. 'But no-one is to leave this room until I have checked their bag. I'll be waiting over there by the door.'

Students scamper. I walk back to my bag.

'Good one, Adam,' one student remarks, rolling his eyes as he walks off. Someone else punches me in the arm and hurls abuse.

I finish getting changed and as soon as I pull on my shirt, I start to feel self-righteous. *Screw them. I don't care if everyone's seen my belly and my moobs (man-boobs) — someone has stolen my wallet! I'm going to get justice.* I'm the last person to leave the room and, as I grab my bag, I spy a wallet between the cracks of the bench. My wallet. It's fallen through the slats and lies there, innocently, among cobwebs and dust at the back of the wall. I reach under and take it gingerly. Great. Now I'm going to have to own up to my mistake. I walk over to Mr Brown, who shrugs his shoulders at me.

'Sorry, Adam,' he says. I pinch the wallet between my fingers. Mr Brown's shoulders relax.

'Someone must have ditched it under the bench, hoping not to get caught,' I offer, feeling the heat rush to my cheeks.

(continued)

'Any idea who?' asks Mr Brown, starting to turn away, keen no doubt to head off for his own lunch.

'Nah,' I say. 'Don't worry.'

Mr Brown nods. 'Okay, get going.'

'Sure,' I reply.

I walk towards the canteen with my bag slung over my shoulder. I'm hot and sweaty from athletics, but I'm also flustered from what happened in the locker room. As I'm walking, a group of three students approaches me. One of them is known in our school for being a dealer and he's with two of his druggie mates.

'Hey, Adam,' he says, as one of his friends shoves me up against a wall. 'You owe me 800 bucks.' His other mate kicks me in the shin, hard.

'Owww!' I yelp, trying to bend forward but getting pushed back.

'You and your stupid bag search!' The dealer leans in close. 'We had to ditch all our gear in the toilet. You owe us.' His friend slams my body against the wall and they walk off. I crumple to the floor, grabbing my shin. It's swollen and turning black and blue already. The pain brings tears to my eyes. I think about the money. I've only been working for a couple of months; there's no way I can afford to repay them.

I arrive home from school to see my oma's dull yellow 1979 Ford Cortina (the car I don't yet know I'll inherit one day) parked in the driveway and a feeling of warmth rushes through me. Walking through the front door, I kick off my shoes and dump my bag in the hallway. Pots and pans clang in the kitchen. Oma is cooking and cleaning (she's always cleaning).

As I walk into the kitchen, Oma walks over to me, embracing my shoulders. 'Hallo Uh-dum,' she says. ('Adam' always sounded like 'Uh-dum' in her still-thick German accent.) 'Do you want something to eat?'

'Hey, Oma,' I say, hugging her back before walking over to the fridge to grab a coke. 'I'm good, thanks.' I pop the can and head towards my room, ready to settle in front of the TV. In the kitchen, Oma finishes cooking a roast chicken, mash and gravy. It's one of my favourite meals. My other favourites are her bread, cream cheese and cucumbers soaked in dressing (I know it sounds gross, but it's awesome!) and her Polish sausages with sauerkraut. Oma also makes the world's best apple crumble.

Before long, Oma pokes her head into my bedroom to say goodbye and then I'm on my own for the evening. A weird feeling in my chest makes me long for her to stay, but I brush it aside. I know she has to go home and look after my Opa.

I serve myself an enormous bowl of roast chicken, mash and gravy with three slices of bread and extra gravy to dunk the bread into. I shovel my dinner into my mouth, savouring every bite of Oma's comfort food.

After dinner, the hours stretch endlessly before me. Dad won't be home until late and the memories of the day begin to loom in my mind. My muscles tense as a familiar sense of dread creeps in on me. I escape it in the only way I know how: watching TV. I start to remember the events of the day; the drone of the TV isn't enough to block out the negative thoughts that are bombarding my mind. I turn to my main coping mechanism — pornography — and I feel numb. Briefly, I feel better. It doesn't last long.

The hours pass. Eventually, I go to bed. Dread lies heavy in the pit of my stomach. I don't want to sleep because I can't face waking up and going to school. It's bad enough getting bullied all the time, but I'll also have to deal with the drug money

(continued)

situation. *Just ignore it*, I think, closing my eyes. But it takes me ages to fall asleep because I'm pinging on sugar and I'm trying so hard not to think about the falsified drug debt. I wished I hadn't said anything about my wallet — then I wouldn't be in this mess. This is typical of me: obsessing about my mistakes for months at a time.

###

Over the next two months, the dealer leaves me alone and slowly I start to forget about it. Then, one day, one of the druggies surrounds me with five of his mates and threatens to bash me after school if I don't pay up.

'I've got 600 dollars,' I say in desperation. 'I'll get it to you tomorrow,' I add, my entire body shaking and sweating.

'Last warning,' says the dealer as his druggie friend plugs me in the ribs, winding me. I'm actually relieved because I feel like I'm getting away with something, but only just. The next day, I withdraw the entire 600 dollars I've saved up while working at the video shop and I give it to him. The dealer nods, pockets the money and walks away. Relief floods my body so quickly I feel like I'm going to pass out. It's over. The dread, the terror, the fear. It's all over.

It took me 20 years to realise I could have had the drug dealer charged with a string of offences. He could have been sent to juvie. Instead, he got paid 600 bucks.

This probably seems pretty obvious to you, but at the time my first reaction was to freak out, so I couldn't think straight.

I didn't have any resilience.

Any time something stressful or challenging happened to me, I'd freak out.

Self-esteem and resilience

During high school, I didn't have a healthy self-esteem. I felt really low about myself and I was always thinking negative thoughts. When my wallet went missing, I immediately assumed it had been stolen instead of thinking to look for it first. Then, when some of the students blamed me for having to flush their drugs down the toilet, I reacted negatively instead of responding in a healthy way.

You

Do you have a healthy self-esteem? When you're faced with a problem, do you automatically freak out and start thinking negatively? Or are you able to think through the problem? Do you feel capable of tackling life's challenges?

Self-esteem and resilience are linked. If you feel good about who you are, you'll find it easy to cope with anything that comes up.

The basketball analogy

In basketball, if you take a shot and it bounces off the backboard and you catch it, it's known as a rebound. While it sucks not getting the shot, it's cool getting a rebound because you've got another chance to score. It's awesome that you get this second chance in basketball — you don't get it in netball. (You also don't get to dribble or steal the ball, and it's also a second-rate sport, but that's another topic.)

(Just kidding. I played one season of netball and I was better at it than I was at basketball!)

If you're resilient, you're like a basketball. You can rebound from the stuff that happens to you quickly and without too much trouble. When life smacks you down, you can bounce right back up. So much so, that the definition of resilience is actually 'your ability to bounce back from the stresses of life'.

Resilience is your ability to bounce back from the stresses of life.

Practice makes better

Basketball training involves repetitive drills and technique work. You need to practise drills to nail your technique. Then, when you're playing a game, the moves come naturally to you and you perform better.

It's the same with resilience. You need to practise and develop the skills. Then it comes naturally to you when you're faced with a problem.

Why is resilience important?

If you're not resilient, you might freak out or get angry at the first sign of stress.

If you are resilient, you can think problems through. You can deal with stress in a healthy way.

Being resilient doesn't mean being fearless. Nor does it mean being tough and *just getting on with things*. It's about:

- understanding your problems
- feeling capable of facing them
- having a strong sense of purpose as you go about it.

Michael Jordan wasn't the GOAT (Greatest Of All Time) at basketball for never missing a shot. He famously said:

I've missed more than 9000 shots in my career. I've lost almost 300 games. Twenty-six times, I've been trusted to take the game winning shot and missed. I've failed over and over and over again in my life. And that is why I succeed.

Michael Jordan knew there was a high chance he'd miss a game-winning shot, but he also knew he could handle failing because it was a positive risk. That's what resilience is all about.

The three stages of resilience

Judith Rodin is a research psychologist who was president of the Rockefeller Foundation from 2005 until 2017. She believes resilience is built through three stages:

1. The Preparation Stage
2. The Responding Stage
3. The Review Stage.

Stage 1: Preparation

Preparing for a challenge means laying out (imaginary) cushions to help you bounce back when you face a challenge in life.

Let me give you an example.

Oma with my son Cale as a baby

When my son Cale was learning to walk, he constantly fell over. Sometimes these were big stacks and he landed on his bottom, but it never bothered him because he always had on a giant, cushioned nappy. Sometimes he'd cry a little in shock. But usually, he'd just get back up and carry on playing.

In comparison, several years ago I owned a motorbike for six months. At the time, I felt as though I was invincible. I thought I would ride for the rest of my life. Six months later, I had a run-in with a cement truck. My foot was crushed between my bike and the truck. For 20 minutes, I was lying on the ground screaming. I couldn't even think about standing up because the pain was *so* bad. Do you think I thought about trying to get off the road? No – I didn't even consider it. I was in too much pain to even think about trying to move.

So what does this example have to do with resilience?

If you're already in pain, it's impossible to bounce back when stressful things happen to you. You can't even *think* about getting up and carrying on. That's why it's important to put cushions in place. You'll still experience falls. We all do. Being resilient means when you do fall, you've got a soft landing. The pain is manageable, and it's easier to bounce back.

You can think of the preparation stage as your drill work. You can prepare yourself by laying down the following cushions:

- Build healthy relationships.

- Learn to understand yourself.

- Challenge negative thoughts.

BUILDING HEALTHY RELATIONSHIPS

Being deeply connected to your friends, family, co-workers and local community makes you live longer. It's true! Taking the time to build healthy relationships makes you healthier.

How many people should you have in your life?

You might have heard of 'Dunbar's number'. Robert Dunbar is an evolutionary psychologist and specialist in primate behaviour. His research shows that we (and our primate ancestors) can only maintain up to 150 relationships at a time. But we don't have the inner resources to provide all of these people with our full time and attention. It would be exhausting. So, how do we know where to invest our energy?

That's where relationship circles come in.

Picture yourself standing in the middle of a large circle. You're surrounded by all of your friends, family members and acquaintances. You can map your relationships across a small, medium and large circle as shown in the relationship circles diagram.

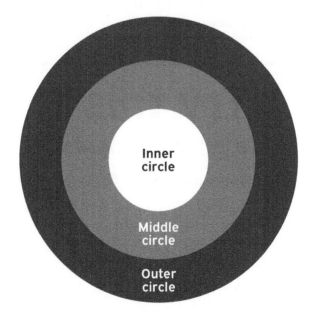

Relationship circles

Relationship circles consist of:

- *an inner circle:* the smallest circle represents your inner circle. These are the people you turn to when times are tough. They are the people you can't imagine life without. You can generally count the number of people in this circle on one hand. You will invest most of your energy into the people in this circle.

- *a middle circle:* this circle usually consists of a mix of friends and family. This is a great circle to look at when you're identifying who you'd like to develop stronger bonds with. You'll usually have up to 10 people in your middle circle.

- *an outer circle:* your outer circle consists of the friends, family, students and community members (think neighbours, teachers, etc.) in your life who you don't interact with as often. The people in this circle still play an important role in your wider social circles but you don't turn to them during times of crisis like you would with those in your inner circle.

Try this
Relationship circles

Draw your own relationship circles. Who falls in your inner circle?

Note: Sometimes students ask me what they should do if they don't have anyone in their inner circle. It's important to work on trust. This is a quality that all relationships require at their core (we'll talk more about this in chapter 10). Begin by reaching out to your middle circle—those people you sort-of trust—even if it's just a little bit.

LEARNING TO UNDERSTAND YOURSELF

We touched on self-awareness in chapter 1, and I've devoted an entire chapter (chapter 6) to learning how to be self-aware. Why? The Ancient Greek aphorism 'know thyself' is the first of the Delphic maxims for a good reason. If you take the time to learn about yourself, you'll know why you're having certain thoughts and why you're feeling a certain way. It's a great resilience tool to have under your belt.

Me

When I was growing up, I wasn't self-aware. I didn't know basketball was an important part of who I was. Every time I played a game and missed a shot it destroyed me. I felt crippled with embarrassment. But I didn't understand *why* I felt so angry at myself.

Now I know myself. I know how much I love basketball. I know winning a game gives me a buzz. I also know I get really competitive and pour all of my heart and soul into a match. That's why I used to feel so devastated when I missed a shot. Now I can reason with myself. I've got the skills to pick myself up from my failures and carry on. I'm so passionate about playing that I won't give up when I fail.

You

Think about the last time you failed at something (it could be playing sport, schoolwork, asking out a girl/guy, cooking an egg, dying in a game, a driving test). How did you feel when you failed? Was there a link between how upset you were and how much you cared?

CHALLENGING NEGATIVE THOUGHTS

If you notice you're having an Automatic Negative Thought (ANT), you have the opportunity to challenge it.

Think about your brain as a map. Your thoughts are the roads. When you catch yourself having a negative thought, and you change it into a positive thought, it changes the physical structure of your brain. A new road is built. This path is called a 'neural passage'.

In high school, I had to study a poem by Robert Frost called 'The road not taken'. Have you read it? The poet comes to a fork in the woods and has to choose which way to go. He chooses the path 'less travelled by' – instead of the path that was well worn – even though the second path would have been easier to walk.

Your brain behaves the same way. Automatic Negative Thoughts (ANTs) are the well-worn neural pathways. If you notice you're having an ANT, you can choose to think differently. The new, less-travelled neural pathway is a path 'less travelled by'. The more often you choose to think the new, positive thought instead of the ANT, the more well-worn the road becomes. Eventually, the new, positive thought becomes automatic and the old, negative thought becomes overgrown before disappearing altogether.

Next time you experience an ANT, picture yourself standing at a fork in the bush or forest and choosing to take the less-travelled road instead of the well-worn one.

Stage 2: Responsiveness

We *will* face challenges in life. We can't avoid problems. The first stage, preparation, was about setting yourself up to face challenges. The second stage, responsiveness, is about managing problems in a healthy way. If you want to be resilient, you need to choose to *respond* to your problems instead of reacting to them.

Me

When I was a teenager, I didn't know how to stay calm and think problems through. I couldn't manage my emotions. My emotions ended up ruling over me. Every choice I made was a reaction to the pain I was feeling. I made two really big mistakes when it came to dealing with my issues:

- *I didn't ask for help:* I tried to push my anger down and my negative feelings away. I didn't realise that ignoring issues doesn't make them go away.

- *I was reactive:* I was in so much emotional pain that every time something happened to me, I became overwhelmed. I reacted in ways that were unhealthy.

Sometimes I would lash out in anger and punch holes in doors and walls.

Usually, I would desperately try to numb my feelings by watching pornography and masturbating or binging on junk food and isolating myself.

BEING RESPONSIVE VERSUS BEING REACTIVE

When something happens to you, you have two options. You can choose to either react or respond.

Reacting means freaking out or getting angry. Remember the wallet story at the start of this chapter? When I discovered my wallet missing, I freaked out. It meant I couldn't be resilient, because I was in a crisis.

Responding means following these four steps:

1. Stay calm and think the problem through.

2. Look at the problem from different angles and come up with different solutions.

3. Mentally follow through the consequences of each solution and decide which one suits you best.

4. Choose what's right, not just what makes you feel good.

If I had responded to my wallet going missing instead of reacting, the outcome might have been very different.

MAKING CHOICES

In high school, most students experience at least a few personal issues. It can be stressful. You have to make a lot of decisions. Sometimes the 'right' decision doesn't immediately give you relief. It can be tempting to do something because it makes you 'feel better', even if this isn't the best decision for you.

When my wallet went missing, I chose to storm off and tell the teacher instead of staying calm. I reacted instead of responding. The idea of getting justice made me feel better.

THE ROLE OF COPING MECHANISMS

It can be tempting to turn towards coping mechanisms during times of stress. Sometimes acting in certain ways or doing specific things helps you feel better. In the wallet story, I was feeling anxious and depressed before my wallet went missing. After being confronted by the drug dealer and his friends, I became overwhelmed and felt like I couldn't cope. I went home and binged on junk food, and watched TV and pornography in an effort to block out my feelings.

Using coping mechanisms is normal. But not all coping mechanisms are created equally. Some coping mechanisms are harmful to your health. Some aren't. Binging on junk food, turning to pornography, drinking alcohol and taking drugs are examples of coping mechanisms that are harmful. Going for a run, hitting the gym, journaling and talking to a friend are examples of coping mechanisms that generally, if done in moderation, aren't harmful to you. These are known as neutral coping mechanisms.

There's nothing wrong with turning towards a neutral coping mechanism if you're working on managing and dealing with your underlying issues. However, it becomes a problem if you choose to use your coping mechanism *instead* of dealing with your issues.

ASKING FOR HELP

If you're going through a problematic time, you need to reach out and ask for help. I didn't know this when I was growing up. I thought I was strong enough to deal with my problems on my own. When the drug dealer and his friends started making threats, I didn't confide in anyone. I turned to my coping mechanisms instead of dealing with the problem.

Sometimes it's hard to know what problems you should ask for help with. There are some things you're capable of working through and managing on your own. That's where the resilience scale comes in. You can use this tool to figure out when you need to reach out and talk about your problems. Before I show you how, let's look at how the resilience scale came about.

Cale's story

When my older son Cale was two years old, I bought him a second-hand trampoline. It was one of those that's surrounded by a net. Unfortunately, the net on this one had a split in it, which I tried (unsuccessfully) to mend with safety pins. I then tried to angle the split towards the grass so that, if Cale came flying out, he'd at least have a soft landing on the grass. This is a photo of Cale, aged 6.

One day I was talking to a friend while Cale was bouncing on the trampoline. I turned around just in time to see him flying through the gap in the net,

(continued)

head first, towards the concrete. Cale didn't know how to put his hands out, so he came crashing down, face first, and started crying. I rushed over and scooped him up. He was screaming and I was crying, thinking *I've broken my kid! This is 'The EPIC Parent Fail!' This is a 10-out-of-10 serious issue!*

The only thing I knew might help to calm Cale down was lollies, so I asked my friend to stay with him while I rushed inside and grabbed a bunch of them. Cale started shoving them into his mouth between sobs. After a while, he calmed down and I could see that, apart from a nasty red bump on his forehead, he was okay. I then thought to myself, *Okay, that probably wasn't a '10-out-of-10' serious issue. Lollies don't fix a 10.*

I decided it was probably a 7 or 8 (mainly because it's never fun to fall on your face). But it wasn't a 10. A 10 is the stuff that takes years to recover from—like divorce, abuse or a death in the family.

This is when the resilience scale was born.

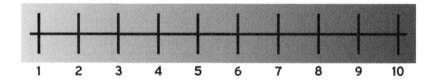

The resilience scale: 1 = low resilience, 9–10 = high resilience

I realised you can measure everything that happens to you on a scale from 1 to 10, with 1 being the easiest problem you might have to face (e.g. 'dying' in an online game).

If it's a 1 or a 2, you can think to yourself, *Hey! Don't let this get to you. Don't sweat the small stuff. You need to shift out of this negative headspace really quickly.* For events that land between a 3 and a 5 you need to get good at dealing with the event on your own.

Once your issues hit anywhere between a 6 and an 8 on the resilience scale, however, you absolutely need to ask for help. If an issue ever reaches a 9 or a 10, you need multiple layers of support. Not just one trusted adult or a couple of friends: you need to be reaching out to as many people as possible, including a psychologist or a counsellor.

After the trampoline incident, I started using the resilience scale with Cale. By the time Cale was seven years old, he had started to get the hang of how to use it. One day, after a year of basketball training, Cale scored seven shots during a training session. At training the following week, he scored none. After training, Cale came running up to me with tears in his eyes.

'I didn't get any shots, Dad,' Cale moaned, tugging on my sleeve.

I took his hand, bent down on one knee and asked him, 'Where is this problem on the scale, buddy?'

Cale looked back at me and answered, his voice unwavering, 'It's a 5?'

I shook my head, resting a hand on his shoulder in an attempt to reassure him and replied, 'No buddy, it's a 1'. Cale's eyes brightened and he turned around, ran back onto the court and started playing line chasey (with himself – as you do when you're seven).

At this stage, Cale knew how to respond to my questions, but he couldn't properly pinpoint where a problem was on the resilience scale.

Two months later, Cale and I went to the Mandurah Crabfest (a family fair day in that town). Cale had some spending money left over from Christmas, so I said to him, 'You can spend it however you like'.

We walked around for ages, Cale inspecting each item for sale at the various art and craft stalls and displays before placing it back down and reconsidering. Eventually, he settled on a squishy mesh stress ball.

'It's so cool, Dad,' Cale announced, running ahead of me and back towards the car. On the way home, Cale was silent, completely obsessed with squeezing his squishy ball. For two minutes, I began chilling out, reflecting on how well the day had gone and how much I'd enjoyed spending time with Cale. Suddenly, out of nowhere, Cale started bawling. I slammed on the brakes and turned my head to look at him.

'Mate, what's up?' I asked, before catching sight of the tiny balls all over the back seat. Cale's stress ball had exploded. Relaxing, I turned back towards the road. 'It's all good buddy, don't stress,' I reassured him, waving an apology to the driver behind me. Cale's sobs slowed to a gradual hiccup before ceasing altogether. 'Well done, bud,' I said, stopping off at the deli to grab him an ice cream. I didn't say anything about the resilience scale.

The next day, I was dropping Cale off at school when he opened the car door and fell out. Yes. He fell out of the car. This kid is as uncoordinated as I am. I jumped out and rushed around to help Cale up off the pavement. A single trickle of blood ran from a shallow graze on his knee. Cale followed my gaze down to his knee before freezing, his face visibly paling before my eyes.

'It's okay,' I said, patting Cale on the shoulder and helping him up. Cale looked up at me, his eyes wide with shock. As he lifted a finger towards the trickle of blood, I noticed a shake in his hand. 'It's all good bud, don't sweat the small stuff.' I smiled at Cale and noticed his shoulders visibly relax as he slowly exhaled.

'Oh, okay,' Cale replied, slinging his backpack over his shoulder. We started walking towards his classroom and, as I bent down to give him a hug, he asked, 'Hey Dad? This morning was a 1 wasn't it?'

I felt my breath catch in my throat: *He got it!* I pushed Cale away and gave him a high five. 'I'm really proud of you!' I announced, feeling a big cheesy grin spread across my face. Cale's eyes lit up and he grinned too. 'And yesterday? That was a zero, right?' he asked.

'My man,' I replied, giving him another hug. Cale had started to place things on the resilience scale for himself.

Stage 3: Reviewing

The final cushion we're going to talk about is called 'reviewing'. This is about using self-reflection to look back on how you dealt with a problem.

Try this
Self-reflection

Once you've successfully overcome an issue, it's vital to reflect on your performance. This involves thinking about the two cushions you had in place: 'preparation' and 'responsiveness'.

PREPARATION

☐ Were you ready to deal with the issue?

☐ Did you have healthy relationships in place?

☐ Were you being self-aware before the problem hit?

☐ Were you actively working on replacing ANTs with constructive, healthy thoughts?

RESPONSIVENESS

☐ Were you able to stay calm at the time the problem arose?

☐ Did you use problem solving to think through a range of solutions?

☐ Did you mentally think through the consequences of each solution before putting one in place?

☐ Did you choose to take action based on what you knew to be right, or did you base your decision on what would make you feel better?

WHY REVIEWING WORKS

By taking the time to reflect on your preparation, you're taking self-responsibility. Reflecting on how you responded to a problem gives you insight and self-awareness.

Resilience is something you can learn. It's about bouncing back from life's challenges and obstacles quickly and with ease. It goes hand in hand with self-esteem and is an awesome tool to have because it puts you in control of your thoughts, feelings and actions. We can't control what's going on around us, but we can control our response – and that's what resilience is all about.

You've got this!

Answer these questions to revise what you've learned about resilience.

1. What does 'being resilient' mean to you?

_____

_____

_____

2. Can you think of a time when something stressful or traumatic happened and you reacted with anger or by getting upset? How did it make you feel afterwards?

_____

_____

_____

3. Can you think of a different time when something stressful or traumatic happened and you responded by seeing the situation as a challenge to be overcome? How did this response make you feel?

_____

_____

_____

4. Do you think having healthy relationships and friendships can improve your resilience? If so, why?

_____

_____

_____

5. What is a healthy way of dealing with your problems?

_____

_____

_____

6. Why are self-esteem and resilience interlinked?

_____

_____

_____

7. Think about someone you consider to be resilient. What is it about them that makes them resilient?

_____

_____

_____

8. An important part of being resilient is choosing what's right when responding to a problem. How could this be easier said than done?

_____

_____

_____

9. What are some tools you could put in place to help you choose what's right, rather than reacting to how you feel?

_____

_____

_____

chapter 3

Bullying

Sadly, bullying is ubiquitous, and it's getting worse. At the time of writing, in Australia, one in four students experiences bullying. If it's something you're going through, you're not alone.

What is bullying?

Bullying isn't just a one-off thing.

By definition, bullying is repeated time and time again.

Bullying is a deliberate, repeated behaviour by someone towards someone else that is designed to hurt, injure or upset the person.

It's different from conflict, where both parties get to express their view equally.

My story

In chapter 1, I spoke about how I used to have low self-esteem. In Year 4, I gained a bunch of weight when I had to start taking medication to treat eczema. Previously, I had been popular at school because I was good at sport. When I gained weight, my sporting ability suffered. Because my self-esteem was low, I was an easy target. I started getting bullied every day.

(continued)

Up until Year 7, I had a small group of friends. There was Andrew, John, Phil and Dan. Andrew was the ringleader of our group. He was loud, freckly and really good at sport. Andrew's dad was coach of the Year 7 soccer team. This gained Andrew major respect in our year. But Andrew had some stuff going on at home that no-one in our year knew about. As time went on, he started getting in trouble at school more often. This photo is of me at age 12, feeling defeated because I wasn't the best runner anymore.

One day, I was playing basketball with my friends and some guys from the soccer team when Andrew decided to play 'Keepy-Off Adam'. Andrew ran off with the ball, yelling at all the other kids to run with him, so I chased them. Even though I'd put on a lot of weight, I was still a fast runner and I quickly caught up. We were all out of breath, puffing and bent over, holding our kneecaps. I turned to my mates, expecting them to crack a smile and laugh, but Andrew had other ideas. He threw a punch in my direction and all the other guys—including John, Phil and Dan—joined in. I ended up with bruised ribs, a black eye and a swollen lip, but the thing that damaged me the most was invisible: my confidence was broken.

The moment my friends turned on me, I lost trust. I was always on edge. I didn't know who I could turn to or rely on, who was my friend and who was just out to get me.

I hoped things would be different in high school. Instead, the bullying just got worse. My first day ended in tears. The story goes like this.

31 January

The aircon is blasting through the car as sweltering heat pummels against the windows. Mum wipes the sweat off her brow with the back of her hand as she gazes at me in the rear-view mirror. It's a Monday afternoon. We're on our way to the uniform shop to purchase our school uniforms. School goes back tomorrow.

'Are you looking forward to starting high school?' she asks. I look up into the wedge-shaped mirror and watch as a bead of sweat collects at the top of Mum's furrowed brow before dropping into her eye. Mum winces and scrunches her eyes closed in annoyance.

'Careful!' my brother yells, as the car begins to veer off the road.

'If I ever make it there.' I answer, smartly, before folding my sweaty arms across my chest and staring out the window. Steam seems to almost rise from the pavement and the quiet neighbourhood street is abandoned, its inhabitants having retreated indoors to the comfort of reverse-cycle air-conditioning, ice creams and watching test cricket on their flat-screen TVs.

'At least you're not going into Year 12,' Paul says, turning around from the front seat to face me. His face is flushed, the shadow of a few scant hairs beginning to reveal themselves above his upper lip. 'I've got mocks and exams, as well as all the normal tests and assignments to deal with.'

I shrug. 'Big deal,' I respond, not bothering to make eye contact with him. Paul is really smart and schoolwork comes easily to him. He'll ace all his exams and probably get into all the top uni courses.

'It's a big year of study for both of you! Things start to get serious now you're going into high school, Adam,' Mum warns. I feel my muscles tense as heat rushes to my cheeks. I clench my jaw in

(continued)

frustration. I don't answer, instead shutting down emotionally. There has always been unspoken pressure in our household to perform well academically. My parents expect me to be as smart as my brother, but they don't realise he doesn't have to deal with getting picked on, beaten up and made fun of all day, every day.

As we pull up in front of the school, which houses the uniform shop, I look around to see if there's anyone I recognise. The familiar knot of anxiety tugs away at my chest and I feel my breath start to quicken. I bite my cuticles, an automatic reaction to being stressed out. What if one of the guys who bullied me in Year 7 is here? I flush with the thought of Mum seeing them rip into me. I don't want her to see me as 'pathetic'.

'Come on Adam!' Mum knocks on my window impatiently. Mum and my brother are standing outside, sweating, waiting for me. I huff and open the door. The air rushes in to meet me. It must be over 40 degrees Celsius out here.

We walk into the school towards the uniform shop, my brother in the lead and Mum following him. I trail behind, taking in the enormity of the buildings, the pathways, the open spaces. It's all so . . . unknown. I'm nervous, but I'm also kind of hopeful. With a new school comes a new start and the opportunity to become a 'new' Adam.

In the uniform shop, Mum picks out shirts, jumpers, pants and shorts for me. Paul already has his clothes; he flashes the special jumper the Year 12s get to wear, as well as his sports uniform. He spies the shorts in Mum's hand.

'Don't get shorts,' Paul warns me. 'No-one wears shorts.'

'Pfft.' Mum looks at Paul and laughs. 'What do you mean "no-one wears shorts?" It's 40 degrees outside. You wouldn't wear pants on a day like today, would you?' Mum asks. I look at Paul, incredulously. I can't imagine wearing long pants in this weather. I'm just about dying as it is.

Paul shrugs. 'Suit yourself,' he says knowingly. Mum gets me the shorts.

1 February

My alarm sounds at 7 am. As I open my eyes, a barrel of emotion tumbles from my brain and lands in my chest with a thud. It's the first day of high school. I'm nervous. I don't know where to go. I don't know where my homeroom is, where my locker is. I don't know my timetable or what books to take. There are a few guys and girls from my year group who I'll know, but they either hate my guts or couldn't care less about me. There's heaps more kids my age who have never met me before. They don't know I'm the class loser and, for once, I'll be completely anonymous. At the very least, they won't torment me and maybe (I'm hesitant to let myself hope, but maybe) I'll make some new friends.

By the time I get up, have a shower and put on my uniform, Dad's already left for work. I cringe as I walk into the kitchen and see Mum packing my lunchbox. Paul is sitting at the kitchen table, eating a bowl of cereal.

'Can't I take lunch money?' I ask, walking over to the fridge, opening the door and gazing at its contents. 'It's so uncool to take a lunchbox.'

Mum slams the butter knife down on the kitchen bench. 'Don't be so ungrateful! Couldn't you at least say good morning?' Paul sniggers. I slam the fridge door closed and storm out of the kitchen. Five minutes into my first day and I'm already in trouble.

I sit in front of the TV watching cartoons and eating my standard breakfast (two Weetbix crushed up with warm milk) until Mum leaves the kitchen to go and have a shower. Then I head to the pantry, grab my lunch plus a couple of chocolate bars and another packet of chips, before Paul and I leave for school.

(continued)

As I traipse down the street, the handles of my backpack tug at my shoulders. It's so heavily loaded with books. My thighs chafe with sweat, my shirt sticks to my stomach and I'm puffing by the time I reach the end of the laneway, where my aunt is supposed to pick us up to take us to school. As I release the bag from my back, it drops with a thud and a few kids from the nearby bus stop look over. I feel like they're looking at the way my shorts bunch between my thighs, or that they can see my fat stomach stuck against my shirt with sweat. Or maybe they're looking at my narrow eyes, magnified underneath my big coke-bottle spectacles. It feels like they're judging me, noticing that I stink of sweat, that my clothes are new and tight, and that I'm standing on my own. Gazing down at my schoolbag, I feel exposed: as though the kids looking at me can see straight into me and see the ugliness, the weakness, the worthlessness.

'Hey Adam!' I look up to see who's calling my name, but no-one is looking at me. I realise that one of the other three Adams from my year is there.

Shortly afterwards, my auntie pulls up beside us and I clamber into the back seat. My cousins Merissa and Narelle are there, but I still feel really lonely.

As I walk into the school listening to the chatter of excited voices around me, I look for a classroom called 'C2'. A piece of paper tells me that's where I need to go for homeroom. Kids are running, yelling, laughing. Girls stand in small clusters, pushing their bodies against each other like penguins. A few girls are left on the outside, looking for a way to push themselves in and be part of the group. Boys push and shove at each other, laughing, joking around, their bags strewn around the grass, as careless as they are. I stand hopelessly, with my heavy backpack, in the middle of the quadrangle, gazing around at the buildings, not knowing where to go. I feel a lump form in my throat as I wish desperately I just had one person to talk to. I hear a familiar laugh behind me.

'Nice shorts!' As I turn, I see Tom, Archer and Matt, three guys from Year 7. They were my friends before Tom decided I was a loser and turned the others against me. They've all changed a bit over the summer break—they look older, bigger, stronger. And they're all wearing long pants. I look down at my pale sausage legs covered in spiky blonde hairs. I'm humiliated.

'Sexy legs, Adam. Did you get yourself a tan?' Matt asks sarcastically, and they all laugh. I turn away, the lump in my throat swelling, threatening to suffocate me.

'Just leave me alone,' I answer, walking randomly towards one of the buildings. I don't know where I'm going—they all look the same. I just want to get away.

'You'll have heaps of fun in the home economics building!' Tom laughs. 'Go sew yourself a pair of real pants! Ones that fit your fat arse!'

The kids around him explode into laughter and I walk away, tears welling, not just because I've been made fun of (I'm pretty used to that by now), but because I'd hoped so desperately for a fresh start, an opportunity to go to school and, just for one day, to blend in and be normal. Already, kids I'd never met before are laughing at me. Already, they've seen me as weak and as an easy target. *It will only get worse from here*, I think despondently.

The bullying triangle

Bullying isn't an isolated incident. It happens when someone who is in a 'position of power' over you repeatedly does things to deliberately upset, injure or hurt you. There are three parties involved when it comes to bullying: the person/people who bully others, the person/people who get bullied and the bystander/s.

What is a 'position of power'?

The word 'power' comes from the Latin *posse*, which means 'to be able to'. If someone is in a 'position of power' over you, they are able to choose to either help you, or to hurt you.

The key word here is 'able'.

For example, you show up to school in a new pair of glasses. Your best friend is able to start making fun of you about your new glasses, but you are able, in turn, to ask your best friend to stop. This is because you see each other as equals. Your best friend isn't in a 'position of power' over you. This isn't bullying.

The class bully, Terry, is also able to start making fun of you about your new glasses, but you might not be able to get Terry to stop. This is because Terry is in a 'position of power' over you. There isn't meant to be an imbalance of power between you and Terry, but this is what Terry wants. Terry is deliberately making fun of you to upset you. If Terry does this repeatedly, it's classed as bullying.

Who else is in a position of power?

Bullying isn't just an interaction between a person who bullies someone and someone who gets bullied. There are third parties involved, known as 'bystanders'. A bystander is anyone who sees, or knows about, bullying happening to someone else. Bystanders are in a 'position of power' over the person being bullied. They can either be complicit in the bullying – even by just standing by and doing nothing – or they can choose to help the person being bullied.

It's important to remember that, by doing nothing, a bystander is supporting the bullying behaviour.

The bullying triangle looks like this:

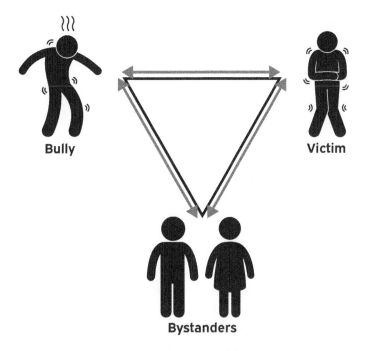

Bully

Victim

Bystanders

The bullying triangle

People who bully others

There will always be people who have a position of power over you in life. Some people are meant to have it. But, just because someone has more power than you, it doesn't mean they are someone who bullies you.

For example, your parents are in charge of you and responsible for making sure you are cared for, looked after and don't get hurt. Your teachers need to tell you what you can and can't do at school, but they're also responsible for teaching you stuff.

There are kids who are bigger, stronger, older, smarter, more popular, better at sports, or have more money and better stuff than you. In turn, you'll always be in a position of power over someone else. You can use this power for good or evil (yes – we're all Marvel characters after all).

Unfortunately, having a position of power means a person has the ability to repeatedly hurt or injure someone who has less power than they do. That's bullying.

People who bully others look for someone who is powerless. They use their position of power to hurt, upset or injure someone who would find it hard to stand up to them.

My story, continued ...

Why did Tom choose me as his target?

On the first day of Year 8, when Tom made fun of my shorts, he chose me as his target because he thought I couldn't stand up to him. Unfortunately, he was right. Despite Paul's warnings, there were other kids wearing shorts (although not many), but Tom directed his comment at me because he thought he'd be able to upset me. Pretend for a moment that Tom had walked up to Dave, a guy in Year 9 who was standing with a group of mates. Let's say Dave has been in high school for a year already, so he knows his way around and has a group of friends.

Tom taps him on the shoulder instead of me and says, 'Hey, nice shorts'.

Weird, right? Dave and his friends might laugh at Tom. Or flat out ignore him. Dave probably wouldn't be as upset as I was so Tom wouldn't feel more powerful. If anything, he'd feel embarrassed.

Tom chose to make fun of me not because I was wearing shorts, but because I was powerless to stand up to him. I was feeling scared because it was my first day and I didn't know where I was going. I was on my own and didn't have the support of any friends. Tom already knew me from Year 7 and he knew he was in a position of power over me.

What was Tom's problem?

Why did Tom want to upset me? Well, by putting me down, Tom was raising himself up. You see, by making me feel powerless Tom was making himself feel more powerful.

Someone might feel driven to make themselves feel more powerful if they are fearful or scared about something, or if they don't feel very good about themselves. Sometimes, when we're feeling really bad, we'll do almost anything to feel better. Tom might have been feeling fearful or anxious about starting high school too. He might even have had stuff going on at home that I didn't know about. The fact is, I don't know why Tom felt bad about himself. At the time, I didn't know Tom was bullying me to make himself feel better.

Bullying is *not* okay

It is *never* okay to hurt, injure or upset someone else just to make yourself feel better. Regardless of what's going on for you in your personal life, you don't have the right to make someone feel bad just to make yourself feel better. *No-one* has that right.

If you are being bullied, I want you to remember a few things:

- You are not the problem.
- You are not alone.
- You can choose to react to the bullying, or you can choose to respond in a healthy way.

You are not the problem

Sometimes your words or actions give a person who bullies others ammunition. This doesn't make the bullying your fault.

For example, in Year 8 I tried to stand up for myself when another student pushed in front of me in line for the canteen. The story goes like this.

My story

How I became Adam 'Bra-zoola'

It's 12.45 pm and I'm standing in the longest queue. Flies buzz around my face, landing on my sweaty forehead, my nose, my eyelashes. I bat at them, annoyed. My shirt sticks to my skin, and my feet feel like they've been shoved into an oven inside my trainers. *Maybe I should just get an ice cream for lunch. It's too hot for a sausage roll.* (We didn't have Healthy Schools canteens back then.)

I'm busy staring at the menu on the board above my head when I feel my body get shoved sideways.

It pushes me off balance, and I yell out, 'Hey!' It's Liam, one of the guys in my year. He's pushed in front of me to join his friends in the line.

'What?' asks Liam, throwing his hands outwards exaggeratedly and looking at his friends. His stomach lurches over the top of his belt, tight against the fabric of his shirt. With his hands outstretched, he's as wide as two of me, and he could take me down in an instant.

'You pushed in,' I say, looking up at his red, sweaty face, feeling my fists tighten.

'So? Whatcha gonna do about it, Bra-zoola?' Liam chides, before cracking up. 'Get it?' he taunts. 'Bra-zoola? Because your last name is Przytula and your boobs are so massive you should wear a bra! Ha ha ha.' It's lame and stupid, but Liam's friends burst out laughing. I feel the blood rush to my face as I become conscious of my so-called boobs taut against my shirt. I hold my ground, ignoring them.

'Bra-zoola? Good one Liam,' says one of the seniors, giving him a high-five. Never mind that Liam's got boobs way bigger than mine.

I remember walking to class feeling like it was my fault I'd earned myself the nickname 'Bra-zoola'. It was because I was overweight. It was because I had a last name that was easy to make fun of. I felt as though I was to blame for the bullying because I was a bad person.

I didn't know that no-one (including me) deserves to be bullied. Or that no-one (including Liam) has the right to bully anyone else.

BULLYING IS HARMFUL

Getting bullied hurts deeply, and it can hurt you permanently. I used to wake up every morning feeling awful. I didn't know it at the time, but I was feeling anxious. Before I even opened my eyes, I was aware of how tight my chest was. How fast my heart was racing. It felt like an elephant was sitting on top of me. It made me feel sick, and I didn't want to get out of bed. I dreaded going to school because I knew I was going to get picked on but I didn't know when it was going to happen.

I didn't tell anyone about the bullying. Instead, I bottled up my feelings. I had outbursts of anger. I couldn't concentrate at school and my grades suffered. My self-esteem plummeted. I felt powerless. This made me a target for more bullying. It got to the point where I felt I couldn't cope.

You are not alone

I know I'm not alone in having felt like this. Students are being bullied in every single class I talk to. Four out of five students think bullying is a huge problem at their school.

Cyberbullying wasn't an issue when I was at school because we didn't have 'socials' (social media) back then. This meant I could escape the bullying when I went home. But I still felt really alone.

These days, it's easier to connect with people online who are going through the same issues you are. But on the flipside, cyberbullying means you literally have nowhere to escape. It can become overwhelming. How do you cope?

Responding/reacting to bullying

There are three possible responses to bullying:

- *the passive response.* This means doing nothing and allowing the bullying to continue. It's not a healthy response. Doing nothing means you take on everything that is said about you. When you hear something said about you often enough, you start to believe it. This is what I did 95 per cent of the time.

- *the aggressive response.* If you choose to fight back, it might be physical or verbal. It's an unhealthy response. Why? You might lose and get hurt. Or you might win the fight and the bullying stops. So then why is it an unhealthy response? Because you learn to react to all your problems with aggression.

- *the assertive response.* If you're assertive, you make a firm request for the bully to stop. It means you're standing up for yourself without being aggressive. Most of the time, telling someone about the bullying and reaching out for help is part of the right response. There's a difference between 'dobbing' on someone and asking for help. Dobbing on someone is done for the purpose of getting that person in trouble.

TALKING ONE-ON-ONE

I know it can seem daunting, but try to speak with the bully one-on-one. This works because when there's no-one else around, you're removing the bully's position of power.

After Liam called me 'Bra-zoola', I saw him again later that day ...

My story, continued ...

I'd excused myself from class to go to the drink fountain. As I left the classroom, one of the students jiggled his hands over his chest. The other students laughed, and I felt my face burn in shame. Clearly my new nickname had spread across the year group already.

My eyes were downcast as I stared at the cracks in the brickwork. I was thinking to myself, *Liam's way more overweight than me. How can he get away with picking on me for my weight?* When I looked up, I felt my body jolt. I could see Liam's unmistakable figure hunched over the drink fountain. I swore under my breath.

Liam turned around. 'Hey, 'sup?' I felt my jaw drop. 'Um.' Liam nodded and walked off.

This would have been the perfect opportunity for me to address Liam one-on-one about the situation in the canteen line earlier that day. Liam acted 'normal' because there was no-one around to see him lay into me. Saying something hurtful or making fun of me wouldn't have made Liam feel any more powerful because he wouldn't have received any recognition for it.

Bullies often act differently without a crowd because the power dynamic is removed. If you are being bullied, try to seek out that person when they are on their own. If they seem to be acting differently, try talking to them on an even keel. Once the person bullying you no longer sees themselves in a position of power to you, the bullying behaviour will stop.

WHO SHOULD YOU ASK FOR HELP?

Growing up, I only reached out for help once. It was in Year 8. Mum had already moved out. Dad was working long hours, but one evening he came home early. I decided to confide in him about the bullying. As I mentioned in chapter 1, Dad was from a generation that brusquely dismissed talking about feelings. When I told Dad about my problem with the bullies at school, he declared, 'Ignore it! Ignore it and it will go away'.

I love my dad, but this was the worst advice he could have given me. 'Ignoring it' is the passive response to bullying, and it doesn't work. The bullying didn't 'go away', and I applied this strategy to all of my problems in life.

If you're getting bullied, it's important to find the right person to talk to. There's a huge difference between talking to someone like, for example, my dad (sorry Dad, I do love you) and someone who has had experience dealing with bullying. The right person will know what to say (things that will actually help) and how to guide you in managing the problem.

Teachers, school counsellors and psychologists, deans and chaplains have been trained in helping students deal with bullying. If you're not sure where to go, start with a teacher you like and trust. Or you can reach out to me at @armedforlife.

YOU MIGHT NEED TO ASK FOR HELP MORE THAN ONCE

This is the mistake I made. I only asked one person for help, and the person I turned to didn't give me the right advice.

It can be discouraging when you build up the courage to talk to someone and it doesn't work out. If it doesn't feel right talking to one person, it's important not to give up. Start small. Walk up to a teacher you get along with after class or during recess/lunch and ask, 'Can I talk to you about something?' Teachers and professionals in a school environment are bound by confidentiality, which means that, unless they're concerned you might harm yourself or someone else, you can trust the stuff you tell them will remain between you and them.

Bystanders

Everyone has a responsibility to do something when they see bullying take place, including you. Edmund Burke, an Irish philosopher in the late 1700s, famously said, 'Evil prevails when good people do nothing'.

So what can bystanders do? They can:

- encourage the people who bully others, or
- nothing – choose not to get involved with the people who bully others, or
- choose to get involved in stopping the people who bully others.

It goes without saying that encouraging someone who bullies other people will make the bullying behaviour worse. If you encourage someone who bullies other people, you are actively harming the person who is being bullied.

So, what about doing nothing and choosing not to get involved? People might choose not to get involved because:

- they are afraid of getting bullied themselves
- they think it's funny
- it's just easier to do nothing.

While it might be easier to do nothing, if you are a bystander to bullying, you have a responsibility to do something. (Remember Edmund Burke's quote above.)

THE BYSTANDER EFFECT

On 13 March 1964, a young woman, Kitty Genovese, was stabbed to death outside her apartment block in New York City. Thirty-eight bystanders living nearby reported hearing or seeing the attack happen, but nobody came to her aid. This is known as the 'bystander effect': we are less likely to help someone in trouble if there are lots of other people around.

The bystander effect happens because it can be all too easy to think, 'someone else will help', or 'there must be someone who is more qualified to do something than me'. You might not want to 'interfere' because you're comfortable where you are. It's hard to step outside your comfort zone, even if you can see someone else being hurt. It's important to remember that by choosing to do nothing, you're encouraging the person who bullies others. This makes you complicit in the bullying.

Instead, stop and think, 'How would I feel in such a situation?' If the answer is 'not good', then you have a responsibility, to yourself and to the person being bullied, to step in and ask the bully to stop.

BEING AN ASSERTIVE BYSTANDER (OR AN UPSTANDER)

When my son Cale was eight, he went to a birthday party for one of the boys in his class. He wasn't particularly great friends with the birthday boy, but when he saw him getting bullied, he knew it wasn't right. Cale went up to the person doing the bullying.

'Hey! Stop it! That's not okay. You need to go away,' Cale said. Cale then sat with the birthday boy to make sure he was okay. Cale wasn't any bigger, stronger, older or in any way more powerful than the person who was bullying, but he saw another kid in need. Afterwards, he told me he'd thought, *How would I feel if it was my birthday and I was getting bullied?* Cale said he knew he'd feel pretty bad, so he knew he needed to step in and help. I'm proud he did.

Cyberbullying

Social media can be awesome. It's a place where you can make connections you wouldn't normally have the opportunity to make. You can share content, find inspiration and get entertained. But even if you try your best to stay safe online and create a positive environment, cyberbullies will find a way to troll you.

To understand why someone cyberbullies, we need to understand what motivates them. When you think about it, it's pretty simple. Being behind a screen offers keyboard warriors a sense of being anonymous. Because they can separate their online reputation from their real-life reputation, they say and do things they wouldn't normally say or do in real life.

Cyberbullying is a behaviour that stems from the same issue as real-life bullying. Usually, the person doing the bullying is struggling with low self-esteem. When a person who's engaging in trolling gets attention from the person they're trolling, or from a virtual bystander, it makes them feel better.

So, what are some actions you can take if you're getting bullied online?

- *Don't react.* The person doing the bullying is looking for a response. You don't need to give them one. If you don't react, you're not giving them the power they crave.

- *Take screenshots.* Collect evidence before anything else. Students often come to me and tell me they're being bullied online. If they've got screenshots of the bullying, it's easier for us to address it because instead of it being one person's word against another's, there's indisputable evidence.

- *Report, block and delete.* If the platform offers you the option to report, do it. Then block and delete the person who's bullying you. This will remove them from their virtual position of power.

- *Tell a trusted adult.* Reach out and tell someone you trust what's happened. Show this person the screenshots you've taken, even if you don't feel you want this person to do anything. Even just sharing what's happened will help you feel supported, and the act of talking it through will help you process any feelings that have come up for you as a result of the bullying.

- *Take a step back.* Remember to balance your screentime and try not to be on your socials too much. Even logging off and taking a walk outside will give you a sense of perspective.

- *Remember: it has nothing to do with you.* It's normal and natural to want to defend yourself when you're feeling attacked, but it doesn't help. Remember the person bullying you has their own issues. Try not to project their comments onto yourself. You don't have to; their hateful words are not yours to own and have nothing to do with you.

I don't envy students who grow up with social media and cyberbullying. When I was getting bullied, at least I could escape the bullying by going home. Now, with technology, there is no escape. Cyberbullying has the potential to chip away at your self-esteem and resilience until you feel as though you can't cope. Some ways you can protect yourself from cyberbullying are:

- Only accept friend requests or follow people you know in real life.

- Know the settings on your devices and the terms and conditions of the platforms you're using.

- Balance your screentime.

- If you see cyberbullying happen, report it. Support the person being bullied and let them know you've got their back.

We're all in it together

We all need to look out for each other.

School can be really stressful. Everyone has problems to face, or issues going on at home or in their personal lives. If you're not feeling good and someone starts making fun of you, wouldn't it be reassuring to know one of your classmates will jump in and stick up for you? Sure it would!

When Tom was making fun of my shorts, for example, it would have made a world of difference to me if another kid had come up and said, 'Hey! Stop it!' Or when Liam was calling me 'Bra-zoola', I wish another student would have told him to 'cut it out'.

If you see someone getting bullied, please step in and say something. Or at the very least, reach out and tell a teacher, school counsellor or someone who can help. You never know, you might just save someone's life. Imagine how much safer the school environment would feel if everyone did this.

You've got this!

Answer these questions to revise what you've learned about bullying.

1. Have you ever been bullied?

   ☐ Yes ☐ No

   If so, how did getting bullied affect how you feel about yourself? If not, can you imagine how it might affect the way you feel about yourself?

   _____

   _____

2. What did you do about the problem when you were bullied? If you have never been bullied, think of someone you know who has been bullied. What did they do about it?

   _____

   _____

3. What do you think you/the person you know should have done differently?

   _____

   _____

4. What are some of the reasons someone might bully another person?

   _____

   _____

5. What could you do as a bystander to help both the person who is getting bullied and the person who is doing the bullying?

_____

_____

6. Is it acceptable to do nothing? Why/why not?

_____

_____

7. Can you think back to a time when you bullied someone? Or are you bullying someone at the moment? Be brutally honest with yourself: why did you feel the need to hurt or upset that person?

_____

_____

    a.   What is the right thing to do?

        _____

        _____

    b.   Could you do the right thing?

        ☐ Yes ☐ No ☐ Unsure

8. If you start getting bullied or start bullying someone else, or if you see bullying happen, who can you talk to about it? Identify at least one person in your life—this person should be a) an adult and b) someone you trust.

_____

_____

9. Can you think of any situations in your life where you've come across cyberbullying?

☐ Yes ☐ No

a. If you answered yes, what role did you play in this situation? Were you:

☐ the person bullying someone else ☐ the bystander ☐ the person being bullied?

b. What was your response?

_____

_____

c. If a similar situation happens again, will you respond differently? In what way?

_____

_____

chapter 4

Stress management

According to prominent psychologist Robert Leahy, the average high-school student today has the same level of anxiety as a psychiatric patient in the early 1950s.

Nearly half (47 per cent) of Australian high-school students feel highly stressed.

Some stress is inevitable (think exams, driving tests, relationship break-ups). While you can't avoid stress altogether, you can manage your thoughts and actions around it. By putting strategies in place to minimise the impact of stress, you'll feel stronger and more capable of dealing with any stressful situations that come your way.

I didn't know about managing stress when I was a teenager. I didn't even really know what 'stress' was. I didn't realise how stress affects you – not just mentally, but physically, emotionally, socially and spiritually as well.

My story

If you've heard my stress management talk at school, you might have heard me talk about the time Steph (a girl I had a crush on) drew a flower 'tattoo' on my hand. The story goes like this ...

It's 9 am on a Tuesday morning and I can hardly keep my eyes open as my Year 12 maths teacher, Mr Montague, scribbles algebraic equations on the board. Steph, who lives just around the corner from my house, is sitting next to me drinking coffee through a straw. Steph's really pretty in the way girls who don't know they're pretty are: she has long blond hair (which she pulls into a ponytail) and hazel eyes magnified beneath giant spectacles. She's not super popular or anything, but she's smart and all the other kids seem to like her.

'You look like you need one of these,' Steph says to me, taking a sip of her coffee. I grunt, feeling my lip turn upwards in a half-smile. Steph always makes me feel really good. She's just nice and kind and funny.

There's a commotion at the front of the room as Tom, one of the kids who bullies me every chance he gets, barges into the classroom.

'Sorry I'm late, Mr Montague,' he announces before pushing past everyone and making his way down an aisle. As Tom passes my desk I gaze downwards at my notebook, hoping to escape his attention. I hear him let off a ripper fart, however, before grinning at me and slumping into his chair at the back of the room.

'Phwoar, who farted? Was that you, Adam?' Tom says loudly. I hear the room fill with laughter as my cheeks begin to burn. It's pointless to deny it.

Steph lays a hand on my arm.

'Don't worry,' she whispers fiercely. I feel the fire of shame and humiliation extinguish.

'Thanks,' I mumble.

As the lesson continues, I start to think about asking Steph if she wants a lift home from school and an internal battle begins:

But what if she says no? part of me argues — the negative, ANT part.

Just do it. What have you got to lose? my more sensible side counters.

Only everything! She won't want to sit next to you in class and you'll look like a total loser!

She won't say no. I'm one of the only guys in this year level who has a car.

Na! Steph wouldn't want to be seen dead in a car with you!

My negative side triumphs. My self-esteem is so low that I can't even bring myself to offer Steph a lift home! (Bear in mind this would save her a 20-minute walk and it's a rainy day too.) The irony is, at the end of class, Steph turns to me.

'Hey! I heard you've got a new ride,' she says. 'Any chance you can drop me off this arvo?'

I'm floored and elated at the same time. 'Yeah, sure!' I reply, trying not to sound too eager.

So, I begin picking Steph up each morning and dropping her home most afternoons. One day, as we pull into her street, I feel Steph's body stiffen beside me.

'What's up?' I ask, glancing over at her stricken face. Steph looks at me. She's biting her lower lip and has her arms crossed over her body. She's vulnerable.

'Dad's there,' Steph replies, indicating a red ute sitting in her driveway. 'Can we turn around?'

(continued)

I swing the car around without questioning her further and hear Steph sigh with relief. 'He moved out a few nights ago,' Steph offers by way of explanation. 'If he's there, my parents will be screaming at each other. I can't deal with it. Sorry ...'

I nod. 'That's cool,' I reply, cranking some tunes in an effort to calm her down. I could open up to Steph and let her know I totally get it—that my parents used to scream at each other too. And that my mum left us too. But I don't have the guts. I'm so scared she'll think less of me or—even worse—feel sorry for me, so I don't say anything. I drive a few more laps of the block and once Steph's dad has left, I drop her home.

At the time, I didn't realise I was being a terrible friend to Steph by not opening up to her and having a real conversation. I was so wrapped up in my own insecurities it didn't occur to me that my personal experiences could actually have been of value to her.

The next day in maths, Mr Montague is writing algebra equations on the board again and I feel Steph tap me on the arm.

Thanks for yesterday, she scribbles on her notepad.

I lean over. *NW*, I write back before looking up at her. 'You okay?' I mouth and she smiles before drawing a flower in her notepad.

Nice tatt! I write next to it, and Steph leans over, carefully replicating her flower drawing on the back of my hand. The feeling of Steph's fingertips resting on the top of my wrist gives me tingles and, as I watch her trace petal upon petal, all I can think about is how crazy I am about her.

As the bell rings to signal lunch, I take my hand back.

'Sweet tatt,' Steph comments, winking at me and I swear to myself I'll never wash it off.

Lunchtime is usually a really stressful time of day for me. As I walk to my locker to dump my books and grab my lunch money, my muscles always tense up and my heart starts racing.

I'm usually thinking, *Who am I gonna sit with? Should I head to the gymnasium? What if my group of 'friends' aren't there? I'll look like a loser. Should I go hide in the toilets? Or just bail and go home?*

Usually, I can feel my every sense — sight, hearing, smell, touch and taste — on high alert and the dread sits like a rock in the back of my throat. Today, with Steph's tattoo carefully drawn on the back of my hand, I feel better. I don't care if Tom and his mates start ripping into me. I'm elated. I feel like I can take on the world.

I find a couple of guys I usually hang out with playing table tennis.

'Hey,' I nod, looking around the gym. "sup?'

'Hey,' they both answer, not bothering to look up from their game. As I rip open the paper packaging and begin to eat my hotdog, Tom and his friends walk past. Tom stops in front of me and gives an exaggerated sniff.

'That wasn't funny,' I remark, in response to Tom's earlier prank in class. Tom smiles.

'Hey, what's that pretty little thing on your hand?'

All of the guys start sniggering then.

'It's 'cos he's gay,' one of them offers, and they laugh. My 'friends' look at me helplessly. There's nothing they can do.

'Adam's a faggot,' Tom announces, his voice carrying around the gymnasium. The other students look over at us and I can feel the heat rush to my cheeks. All of a sudden, I can't swallow. The air sticks to my lungs like quicksand and it feels like the floor, the walls, the ceiling begin to cave in on me. My heart is racing and every fibre in my body is ready to flee but my mind

(continued)

stays frozen as I stare at the stupid, pathetic loops of the flower cursively strewn across my hand.

'Get lost!' I manage. The words roll thickly from my mouth, sounding foreign and hollow in my ears. Tom doesn't even hear me. My friends stand there dumbly, not wanting to be a target and besides, what can they do? Eventually, Tom and his friends are lured away by the giggles and pointed looks of a group of girls. As they walk away, I feel my muscles relax and I can finally exhale. I leave the gym, walking briskly to the toilets and scrub at the flower drawing, swallowing the lump in my throat and willing the hot salty tears to stay in my eyes rather than escaping down my cheeks. Steph will definitely notice it's gone when I drive her home. I'll just have to act tough and tell her I washed it off because it was stupid.

What does my story have to do with stress?

As a teenager, I had no real understanding of what stress was. I thought stress was just 'in my mind'. I assumed being stressed was always a bad thing. I was always stressed out. It affected my mental health and my physical health. It wasn't just the bullying making me stressed. There were other factors too, such as:

- *the other students at school* – because they either bullied me or laughed along with the person bullying me

- *going to class* – because I couldn't concentrate and was starting to fall behind with my grades

- *recess and lunchtime* – because I couldn't predict what was going to happen and I didn't know if I'd have anyone to sit with

- *my home life* – Mum had moved out, Dad was working long hours and I felt stressed being on my own most of the time

- *spiders* – those terrifying creatures show up everywhere.

You

You're probably feeling stressed as well. At least from time to time. Most of us are. It's most likely not for the same reasons that I was feeling stressed. The stress response is the same regardless of what causes it. This chapter will help you respond to stress in a healthy way.

What is stress?

The definition of stress, according to Headspace (an Australian non-profit organisation for youth mental health) is:

A physiological response that triggers the autonomic nervous system, leading to a spike in the release of epinephrine and cortisol – the stress hormones.

If you love science and you study human biology, you're probably all over this definition. If not, the takeaway is *stress is a physical response. It's not just 'in your mind'.*

Stress is a survival mechanism

When you're stressed, your body throws all its resources into getting you moving. Your heart pumps faster to get your blood moving. Your body even sends glucose to your muscles to get them working faster.

The fight-or-flight response

Picture this: it's a hot summer's day and you've hit the beach with a mate for a surf.

You're paddling out, the water is cool and refreshing and there's an awesome swell.

Next minute — dah-doom ... dah-doom ... dah-doom-dah-doom-dah-doom — there's a big black shadow in the water. Your muscles tense, your heartbeat can be heard all the way across the ocean. Your brow starts sweating, your vision gets blurry. With a yelp, you jump up onto your board.

'Shark!' you yell, and your mate leaps up onto his board ...

What do you do?

- *fight* — kick, punch and defend yourself
- *flee* — paddle for the shore as fast as you can
- *nothing* — freeze and hope the shark doesn't see you.

Which one did you choose?

I hope you chose to paddle like crazy because I think you'd be mad to front a shark! And I don't know about you, but I wouldn't want to wait around to get eaten.

'Fight-or-flight' is your body's physiological response to danger.

When you're in fight-or-flight mode, you can tap into heightened abilities to help you survive. (You basically turn into a superhero.)

Note: Sometimes, the 'fight-or-flight' response is referred to as the 'fight-or-flight-or-freeze' response. Usually, it's easier to just say 'fight-or-flight'.

In the shark scenario, if you had chosen the 'fight' response, you would have been stronger, faster and put up a better performance than if you'd just been play-wrestling with a friend.

If you had chosen the 'flight' option, you would have been able to paddle faster and harder than ever before.

If your instinct was to 'freeze', your heightened focus may have given you a higher chance of survival than if the stress response wasn't triggered by you seeing the shark.

Fight-or-flight is a physiological response

The fight-or-flight response is your body's reaction to danger. It allows you to react quickly to a threat through the activation of your sympathetic nervous system (SNS). The fight-or-flight response isn't a bad thing. It helps you fight off sharks.

But it's only meant to last long enough to get you out of a stressful situation.

Back in the day, your ancestors relied on the fight-or-flight response to survive. They might have had to fight off enemies with spears. Today, we live a more comfortable life. We don't often come across sharks (unless we're playing Fortnite Chapter 2, Season 3). But most of us stress too much.

Some of us live in a constant state of stress. This can have a nasty effect on our bodies.

Let's talk science

To understand the fight-or-flight response, you need a basic understanding of your body's nervous system.

WHAT IS THE NERVOUS SYSTEM?

Your nervous system is made up of your brain, spinal system and nerves. It's your body's communication system. The nervous system carries messages to and from your brain to other parts of your body.

The nervous system has two main regions: the central nervous system and the peripheral nervous system.

We're going to be talking about the peripheral nervous system.

THE PERIPHERAL NERVOUS SYSTEM

The peripheral nervous system includes all of the nerves that branch out from our brain and spinal cord and extend to other parts of our body, including muscles and organs.

The peripheral nervous system is divided into two parts: the somatic and the autonomic. Let's take a look at the autonomic nervous system.

THE AUTONOMIC NERVOUS SYSTEM

'Autonomic' refers to the part of the nervous system that works 'automatically', without our conscious effort. It's the part of our nervous system responsible for controlling our internal organs.

The autonomic nervous system is further broken down into two classifications:

- the sympathetic nervous system (SNS)
- the parasympathetic nervous system (PNS)

WHAT DOES THE SYMPATHETIC NERVOUS SYSTEM (SNS) DO?

The SNS prepares the body for stress. It's the system responsible for 'fight-or-flight'.

The sympathetic nervous system is like a car's accelerator. If we're suddenly confronted with a threat, the SNS slams on the accelerator and gives our body a surge of energy to help us survive. It does this by triggering our adrenal glands to release hormones, including adrenaline, noradrenaline and cortisol.

When this happens, we tend to experience the following symptoms:

- feeling dizzy or lightheaded
- tense neck and shoulders
- breathing fast and shallow
- nervous poos
- cold, clammy hands
- 'jelly legs' or shaking muscles
- dilated pupils
- dry mouth
- heart palpitations
- 'butterflies' in your tummy
- sweating
- sense of 'impending doom'.

WHAT DOES THE PARASYMPATHETIC NERVOUS SYSTEM (PNS) DO?

If our sympathetic nervous system is our car's accelerator, we can think of the parasympathetic nervous system as our car's brakes. It's what returns our body to homeostasis (a chilled-out state).

Interesting fact: it takes adrenaline a little while to leave our body because, back in the day, enemies with weapons (hunters with spears/ sabre-toothed tigers) would often return. If we're constantly in fight-or-flight mode, our PNS can't return our body to its baseline.

Chronic stress leads to overexposure of the stress hormones, and this can affect all of our body's processes. If you're experiencing chronic stress, you might feel like you're literally just trying to survive.

WHEN IS THE FIGHT-OR-FLIGHT RESPONSE USEFUL?

The symptoms associated with being in fight-or-flight mode could result in you feeling 'not good'. But this doesn't mean the fight-or-flight response is a bad thing. As we've seen, it helps us survive when our life is in danger. It's also useful in everyday life. For example:

- The fight-or-flight response gives us a competitive edge by making us run faster and jump higher when we're competing in sports/athletics.

- Being in fight-or-flight might help us ace a test or exam by allowing us to think more clearly, focus and concentrate.

Did you know that the feeling of 'stage fright' is actually the fight-or-flight response kicking in?

THE PROBLEM WITH FIGHT-OR-FLIGHT

Periods of acute (short-lived) stress are fine. We can enjoy the benefits of having the fight-or-flight response kick in during stressful situations to help us perform better. However, when we experience the symptoms of fight-or-flight continually and over a long period of time, it does more than make us feel stressed out. It actually changes our brain chemicals. It also changes the way our body and mind function. This is known as 'chronic stress'.

Types of stress

There are two types of stress: external stress and internal stress.

External stress refers to the situations in life we have no control over—for example, school tests and exams, relationships, public speaking, spiders, elephants, moths. (Yes, I've met someone who was petrified of moths. I mean, come on, really?)

Internal stress is literally that. It's the stress our body is under on the inside. We can't control external stress, but we can control how much stress our body is under internally. If we can control our internal stressors, then we'll find it easier to manage the external stressors we face each day.

Internal stress and acute inflammation

Inflammation will make our body internally stressed. Inflammation happens when our body tries to fight against something that's harming it. We might have an infection, illness or injury.

Acute inflammation is a good thing. Without it, our body wouldn't be able to heal. Here's a personal story that will help you understand what I mean.

My story

As I'm sure you've gathered, I love playing basketball. There's nothing better than getting possession of the ball, getting open for a shot and taking that jumper. I'm on a pretty good team and a couple of years ago we were playing the team on the top of the ladder.

There were two minutes left on the clock and we were winning by one point when I got a defensive rebound. As I went to dribble, one of the guys on the other team, who was twice my size, ran into me so hard I went flying. I landed on my ankle and it swelled up so much the doctor sent me for x-rays because he was convinced it was broken.

It wasn't, but I did tear a ligament. If you've ever sprained your ankle, you'll know it's painful, it sucks and it's annoying. My ankle was painful, hot and swollen and I couldn't put weight on it. The swelling went down after a couple of months. The injury had completely healed within about 18 months (it took a long time because of bone bruising).

(continued)

My ankle was hot and swollen because my body sent blood and water to the area to try to heal it. In this instance, acute inflammation helped me to recover.

Chronic inflammation happens when the inflammatory response lingers, leaving your body in a constant state of alert.

So why does inflammation make our body internally stressed?

LOWERED IMMUNITY

When we're stressed out, our body releases too much cortisol. This dampens our immune system, and lowered immunity can result in us getting sick more often. When we get sick, our body releases more cortisol to try and lower the inflammation. As you can see in this illustration, this creates a stress cycle:

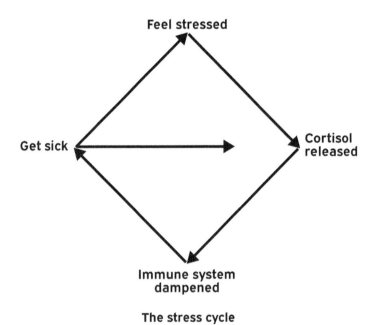

The stress cycle

Our body sees illness as a threat/invader. It goes into fight-or-flight mode and more cortisol is released. Chronic stress causes chronic inflammation, and chronic inflammation causes chronic stress. It's a difficult cycle to break free from. The only way to do it is by making healthy lifestyle choices and managing our internal and external stress. We'll look at strategies for this later in the chapter.

Effects of stress

How does stress affect us physically? Being stressed out affects our hormones. It also affects our brain chemistry. Chronic stress causes:

- high cortisol
- low serotonin.

When we are in fight-or-flight mode, our adrenal glands release cortisol into our bloodstream. If we're constantly stressed out, too much cortisol will be released into our body. This affects both our brain and our gut.

Being stressed out all the time can actually shrink our brain. Wait ... what?

High cortisol

High levels of cortisol can shrink our prefrontal cortex (the part of our brain that influences decision making, judgement, behaviour and concentration).

Increased cortisol can also affect the hippocampus by damaging its electrical signals and preventing new cells from being formed. The hippocampus is responsible for learning and memory. This is why stress can affect our grades. If we're stressed, we can't concentrate, remember stuff or learn new things.

Cortisol also slows down our digestive system. When our body goes into fight-or-flight mode, we might even feel the urge to do a 'number two' because adrenalin relaxes our anal sphincter (that nervous poop is never fun). Chronic stress can make us crave energy-dense carbs and comfort foods. It can also lead to weight gain.

For example, a few years ago, I went through a period of huge stress with my divorce. Every night I'd smash a bag of Pods, a box of Maltesers and a litre of coke. My body was craving these energy-dense foods because my liver was releasing so much cortisol. I gained a bunch of weight, felt sick all the time, my business suffered and I hated on myself even more.

Low serotonin

Neurotransmitters allow our neurons to communicate with other parts of our brain. They also enable our brain to communicate with our body. Serotonin is an important brain chemical that does a lot of work in our gut as well. It helps us feel full after eating and keeps our appetite in check. In our brain, serotonin promotes feelings of wellbeing and happiness. It also plays an important role in helping us to sleep and in balancing our internal clock.

Ninety-five per cent of our body's serotonin is made in our gut and the other 5 per cent is made in our brain. If we're stressed out, our body can't make the serotonin we need to feel good. As a result, we may:

- struggle to stay calm
- feel depressed and anxious
- have rigid, obsessive thoughts and expect perfection
- feel angry and afraid for no particular reason.

Try this

Identify your stress symptoms

How stressed are you? Tick each of the statements that apply to you.

- ☐ I frequently feel angry or irritable.
- ☐ I have constant anxiety.
- ☐ I feel moody or easily frustrated.
- ☐ I regularly feel the need to cry.
- ☐ I lack self-confidence.
- ☐ I often have trouble concentrating.
- ☐ I feel restless most of the time.
- ☐ I constantly feel fatigued and tired.
- ☐ I have trouble sleeping.
- ☐ I often feel nauseated or sick to my stomach.
- ☐ I often experience constipation or diarrhea.
- ☐ I experience frequent headaches or migraines.
- ☐ I have frequent muscle cramps or twitches.
- ☐ I often feel dizzy or faint.
- ☐ I get sick all the time.

YOUR SCORE

If you ticked any of the boxes above, you may be struggling with managing your stress levels.

(continued)

WHAT YOUR SCORE MEANS

If you have symptoms of stress, don't stress!

First, the effects of stress on your body and mind are reversible.

Second, you can use stress to your advantage.

Let's look at some strategies for coping with stress in a healthy way.

Just a quick note: if you're experiencing ongoing mental or physical health symptoms, it's important to get these checked out by a medical practitioner. Sometimes, stress is a symptom of an underlying medical condition, and some illnesses can make stress symptoms worse.

Healthy ways to manage stress

Managing your stress is about making proactive decisions about your physical and mental health. Choosing the following behaviours will have an immediate and direct impact on how stressed you're feeling:

- Eat well.
- Get moving.
- Get 8–10 hours of quality sleep every night.
- Talk to someone.
- Take time to relax.
- Manage your time well.
- Take time out.
- Be positive.
- Accept the things you can't change.
- Stop using coping mechanisms.

Let's look at each of these stress-busting tools in detail.

Eat well

I could write an entire book on this topic. What we eat has a huge effect on how stressed we feel.

EAT MORE PROTEIN AND FAT

One of the symptoms of chronic stress is feelings of depression and anxiety.

High-protein foods assist in the production of serotonin, one of the brain's 'happy' chemical. If you load up with healthy sources of protein, you can boost your body's production of a natural antidepressant. How does this work?

As I mentioned earlier, 95 per cent of serotonin – the brain's 'happy' chemical – is produced in your digestive tract. Tryptophan, an essential amino acid, is the building block of serotonin.

Tryptophan is used to make niacin, which is essential in the production of serotonin. Tryptophan is found in high-protein foods such as:

- free-range chicken
- grass-fed, ethically killed red meat
- wild-caught fish
- free-range eggs
- nuts
- legumes and beans.

I recommend free-range, ethical sources of meat because some studies suggest animals brought up or slaughtered in stressful situations have high levels of inflammation that are passed on to us when we consume them.

For more information on the effect of your diet on your mood, I recommend reading *The Mood Cure* by Julia Ross.

EAT FRESH, UNPROCESSED FOOD

Some foods have an inflammatory effect on our body. This means our immune system is activated, and we have an inflammatory response. Some foods are anti-inflammatory. This means they reduce the inflammation and, in turn, the cortisol levels in our body.

Sugar and salt have an inflammatory effect. Processed foods, refined carbohydrates (white bread, pastries, etc.), fried foods, sodas, processed meat and saturated fat (butter, lard) all cause inflammation. As a result, these foods can make us feel more stressed.

Anti-inflammatory foods include:

- avocado
- olive oil and coconut oil
- green, leafy vegetables such as kale and spinach
- nuts and seeds
- fatty fish such as salmon, tuna and sardines
- some fruits including strawberries, blueberries, cherries and oranges.

I'm not a nutritionist so I can't advise you personally on what you should and shouldn't eat. The key players in the functional medicine field I follow are @drjoshaxe, @dr.tomobryan and @drmarkhyman. Check them out on Instagram.

DRINK WATER

Dehydration causes an inflammatory response. You should drink at least 8 to 10 cups of water per day. This will have a direct impact on your internal stress levels and how stressed you feel.

Me

As you know, my diet wasn't always healthy. When I was in high school, I ate junk food pretty much constantly. I was already under a lot of external stress with the bullying and conflict in my home life. Smashing chips, chocolate and soft drink made me feel better temporarily. I didn't know that what I was eating was causing an inflammatory response in my body and contributing towards how stressed out I was feeling.

Now I'm all about the 80/20 rule when it comes to eating: if I eat well 80 per cent of the time, then I can have whatever I like the remaining 20 per cent of the time (I love McDonald's).

I like to keep my diet pretty simple. I try to make sure my plate is made up of 50 per cent plants/complex carbohydrates (fruit and/or vegetables, and unprocessed grains), 25 per cent meat/protein and 25 per cent healthy fats.

I'm not going to lie: I don't love vegetables. But I know how important they are if I want to feel really good. For example, tonight my wife Cherith and I are having a vegetarian night. We're making a haloumi vegetable stack. It's comprised of haloumi, capsicum, sweet potato and asparagus.

I stack the vegetables, sprinkle them with herbs and balsamic vinegar and pop them in the oven to roast. It's quick, so easy and it tastes really good. Cherith and I have a vegetable and herb garden in our backyard and I'm really enjoying using our own capsicums, tomatoes, raspberries and blueberries. I've also got basil, thyme, oregano and parsley growing. If you want to be inspired by some more of my favourite go-to meals, check out the next page.

My favourite recipes

Breakfast

Turmeric eggs (eggs, turmeric, basil, parsley—fresh if possible)

Bacon with stewed tomato and basil (instead of tomato sauce)

Healthy muesli and coconut yoghurt with fruit (optional)

Protein shake (with almond milk)

Omelette with capsicum/bacon/tomato

Protein pancakes with stewed berries

Chicken broth

Avocado and cherry tomatoes with lemon juice on sourdough/keto toast

Lunch/dinner

Chicken and veg soup

Sausages and sauerkraut

Fried red emperor and salad

Roast chicken and vegetables

Chicken parmigiana and salad

Beef stir fry

Steak and salad

Prawn stir fry

Mediterranean chicken with quinoa and tomato/cucumber

Chicken lettuce cups

Coconut chicken tenders and grilled broccolini

Lamb burgers

Asian pork and rice
Roast chicken (free range) and salad

Fancy meals (I cook these for date nights)

Homemade oysters Kilpatrick
French lamb cutlets and sweet potato mash
Seared barramundi and sautéed capsicum

Vegetarian

Macadamia pesto zoodles
Eggplant parmigiana and vegetables
Vegetable frittata
Zucchini lasagne
Pumpkin soup (with homemade or keto bread)
Zoodles and passata
Jackfruit and slaw burgers

Sides

Baked zucchini (with nutritional yeast)
Sauerkraut
Cajun greens
Roast vegetables
Broccoli with paprika
Grilled garlic asparagus
Sautéed Brussels sprouts with grass-fed butter

Desserts

Apple crisp
Oven baked figs with coconut yoghurt
Paleo brownies/cookies with coconut yoghurt/dairy-
free ice cream

Get moving

When we experience stress, our body releases chemicals to prime it for fight-or-flight. If we don't use this surge of energy, it remains in the body as tension. Regular exercise is vital for releasing built-up tension in our body – and going for a walk isn't enough. We need to do something that mimics survival (such as fleeing a lion or fighting off a shark). That's why resistance training and running are both so effective in relieving stress.

Personally, I prefer weight-based training over running. Why? Running puts a lot of stress on our body. Especially long-distance running done over a long period of time. High-intensity exercise triggers our brain to release hormones called endorphins, which:

- release tension
- make us feel good
- reduce pain
- improve our sleep
- boost our immune system
- reduce inflammation.

Exercise is also a natural antidepressant because working up a sweat stimulates the production of serotonin, the 'happy' chemical. Exercise won't make our problems completely disappear. What exercise *will* do is dial down a notch the intensity of the stress we're experiencing.

When it comes to exercise, remember not to take it to extremes. If you like running, then go for it, but don't only run. If you enjoy lifting weights, go for it, but don't only lift weights and neglect your cardio fitness. Movement is about balance, and that means getting a good combination of resistance and cardio training. See the next page for some of my go-to exercises for combating stress.

My go-to exercises for combating stress

You can find instructions on how to do any of these movements on Google. If you're new to training, I recommend consulting a professional prior to trying any of these out.

Legs
Squats
Split squats
Lunges
Deadlifts
Single leg hip raises
Hip thrusters
Calf raises
Donkey kicks
Glute bridges
Side lunges

Chest
Chest presses
Incline chest presses
Decline chest presses
Press-ups
Diamond press-ups
Shuffle press-ups
Chest flys

Back
Supermans
Back rows
Bent-over reverse flys
Chin-ups
Single arm rows
Inverted rows
Renegade rows

Shoulders
Overhead presses
Arnold presses
Milk pours
Lateral raises
Front raises
Bent over lateral raises
Upright rows

(continued)

Arms	Core
Bicep curls	Planks
Hammer curls	Plank shoulder taps
Zottman curls	Side planks
Dips	Dead bugs
Tricep kickbacks	Boats
Plank shoulder taps	Russian twists
Up-down planks	Bicycle crunches
	Reverse crunches

Get 8–10 hours of quality sleep every night

Did you know that elephants only sleep for two hours each night?

And that dolphins sleep with only half of their brain at a time so they can be alert for predators?

Cool, huh? Humans, however, need 8–10 hours of quality sleep each night. This is because we have complex brains that rely on rapid eye movement (REM) sleep to make memories and learn new things.

Melatonin is the hormone that controls sleep. Melatonin is made from serotonin. You already know you need to eat well and exercise to produce serotonin. You also need at least eight hours of good quality sleep each night to allow your body to recover from physical and mental illness, injury and trauma. Sleep is vital in reducing inflammation and managing internal stress.

WHAT DOES MELATONIN DO?

Your body releases melatonin in response to darkness. Melatonin's job is to help you sleep. It also plays an important role in regulating your circadian rhythms (your body's internal clock). When melatonin is released into your body, you start feeling drowsy.

Your lifestyle plays an important role in either encouraging or discouraging melatonin production. To understand this, you need to think back to Paleolithic times, where humans rose with the sun and went to sleep at dark. Amber and red lighting is ideal for evenings because it has a low colour temperature – similar to a sunset. Red-based lights, candles and Himalayan salt lamps all encourage melatonin production. On the flipside, your electronic devices are backlit by a blue light. Phones, TVs, tablets and laptops all emit a blue-based light that your body relates to the blue skies of daytime. This is why your electronic devices can interfere with the process of simulating melatonin production.

Caffeine can also suppress the production of melatonin. While a coffee in the morning might help you feel wakeful for your day, it's not so helpful after 3 pm.

So, what does this mean?

At least half an hour before bedtime, turn off your electronic devices, put your phone away and switch on a red-light-based lamp/light. Chill out with music, a book and a cup of herbal tea or spend some time meditating or praying before bed. I highly recommend looking up a TED Talk by Matt Walker called 'Sleep is your superpower'.

Talk to someone

If you're feeling stressed out, you need to talk to someone. Just the act of talking can sometimes help relieve tension or stress. It also means you can get a different perspective on a problem. And you can get advice if you need it.

There's also a physiological component to talk therapy. Talking about what's stressing you out can help re-wire your brain. In the same way being stressed can kill brain cells, talking about stress can create new brain cells.

HOW DOES TALK THERAPY WORK?

You might have heard the term 'neuroplasticity'. 'Neuro' translates to 'nervous system' (your brain and spinal cord) and 'plasticity', well, did you ever play with plasticine as a kid? You can bend, stretch and manipulate it in as many ways as you can imagine. What this means is that, by talking to a school psychologist, teacher, chaplain or trusted adult, you can actually build new neural connections in your brain.

That's why it's important to get counselling or talk therapy. It can make you feel less tense quickly and it also helps your brain to function at its best.

Take time to relax

Remember how I mentioned earlier that the sympathetic nervous system is like your car's accelerator, and the parasympathetic nervous system is your car's brakes? You need to press on the brakes sometimes to allow your body to return to its homeostatic state.

Regardless of how much external stress you're facing, it's important to find time every day to relax. This will keep your internal stress low. It will make you feel less stressed overall. Practising relaxation will also help you to cope with external stress.

HOW TO RELAX

Focused breathing and meditation are important. You might think of Buddhist monks or yogis sitting with their legs scrunched up, making 'om' noises when you think of meditation. This is a type of meditation, of course, but it might not be the type that works for you. There are other ways of relaxing too. Being in nature, getting fresh air and going to the beach come to mind.

DEEP BREATHING

Meditation is about deep breathing. When you meditate, you sit still and listen to your thoughts without judging them. This practice reduces your cortisol production. By doing this, you'll get a boost to your immune system and an overall sense of calm and wellbeing.

When I meditate, I focus on my breathing. I breathe in for five seconds, hold for five seconds and breathe out for five seconds. I do this over and over, for as long as possible. I'm also a Christian, and I use prayer to help me relax. There are lots of different breathing techniques online. Alternatively, you can head to a yoga or Pilates class for some guidance. Try to meditate, using a method that works for you, at least once a day – ideally in the morning when your cortisol is naturally at its highest.

Manage your time well

You know that feeling when you're gaming or scrolling through Insta and you suddenly realise two hours have passed? But the next day, you might be sitting in class, staring at the clock and double English just seems to drag on forever?

Time is difficult to manage because our perception of it changes depending on the situation. It's normal to find it really challenging to get things finished on time. This can make us feel stressed.

Here are some really good ways to take control of your time:

- *Categorise your tasks:* You need to accept that you can't do everything at once. You have to prioritise how important each task is. You can categorise everything you need to do as either 'urgent', 'important' or 'whenever'.

  Complete your urgent tasks first, then move on to the important ones before finally hitting the 'whenever' tasks.

- *Plan ahead:* I'm a 'calendar and lists' kind of guy. I use the calendar on my phone to allocate time. I use the Reminders app to write down everything I need to do. My wife Cherith, however, uses a physical diary. That's cool too. Use whatever works for you.

- *Build fat into your time:* Make sure you give yourself more time for things than you think you'll need. That way, if a task takes longer than you estimated, you won't feel stressed. I've found that since becoming a parent, I've had to get good at something called 'backwards maths': counting back from the time I need to leave and thinking about *all* the things I need to do. Then adding some extra time because there will inevitably be a few things I need to do before I leave that I've forgotten to account for. I really suck at this at times because I try to do too much.

Take time out

Think about something you love doing and find time to do it (so long as it's healthy for you). If you can't think of anything, then just take some time to relax. Get some fresh air, eat something healthy and do some exercise. Alternatively, you might want to hang out with some friends. Or spend a night in watching Netflix.

For me, I love hitting the gym, going to the movies and getting a sports massage.

It's really important to take time out to engage in hobbies and activities you enjoy, so long as they're things that are good for you.

TIME WITH YOUR TRIBE

Schedule time to spend with the people you love, or those you turn to for connection. This time should be spent in person, where possible, not just on messenger or socials. Staying connected on your socials is valuable, but it doesn't replace the mental-health benefits you get from actually being physically present with your inner circle, whether they are family, friends or a combination of both.

Be positive

There will always be stressful situations in your life. Exams, relationships, a pet dying, no internet connection – just to name a few. What matters is how you respond to the stress.

A few months ago, I was driving to the airport to catch a flight when one of my car tyres burst. This was a moment of intense stress (I hadn't changed a tyre for 12 years). Instead of completely freaking out and having a meltdown on the side of the road, I pulled over, took a deep breath and thought, *How do I deal with this?*

I decided to stay chilled and I made a plan of attack by doing a quick YouTube search. Instead of letting ANTs take over, I thought to myself, *I've got this.* By taking charge of the situation and choosing to respond positively, changing the tyre on my car in record time and getting on that plane became a challenge instead of a crisis. I was able to use the fight-or-flight response to focus, think clearly, remove the busted tyre and mount a new one. Then I raced (within the speed limit of course) to the airport. I made it to the check-in counter one minute late, but the lady behind the counter let me through and I got on the plane just in time. Once I was in my seat, I popped my headphones in, listened to some music and chilled out.

My body was allowed to return to its normal physiological state, and I felt good.

I was able to deal with having a flat tyre because of YouTube, but also because I had the inner resources to do so.

Accept the things you can't change

There will be some situations that are simply out of your control. About 90 per cent of what you're feeling anxious about will never happen. A further 5 per cent are events you have no control over.

You can't control the people around you, and you can't avoid external stressors like school exams, driving tests, public speaking and spiders. But you can see these things as challenges and use your knowledge and skills to overcome them. You can learn to accept your failures and mistakes, and move on.

Stop using coping mechanisms

Try not to use your coping mechanisms too much. These behaviours become a crutch you tend to lean on rather than dealing with what's actually causing your stress. Negative coping mechanisms tend to increase internal stress and make your hormones go haywire because they rely on activating your dopamine response.

Here are some healthy ways to relieve stress:

- *exercise* – including sport, weight-based training, yoga, Pilates
- *spend time with friends or family* – or even pets
- *relax* – have a bath, do some deep breathing exercises, walk in nature
- *journal* – write things down (including what you're grateful for)
- *listen to music* – classical music, or whatever you enjoy
- *get creative* – dance, build something, design something
- *do some art therapy* – drawing, colouring, painting
- *read a book* – not something for school, but a book you enjoy
- *stimulate your brain* – mentally challenging games; study something you're interested in
- *meditate* – take a meditation class, pray, get outside
- *take a supplement* – examples of stress-busting supplements are omega-3 fatty acids, kava, green tea, lemon balm, ashwagandha (but check in with your health practitioner before taking anything)
- *find a way to laugh* – hang out with a friend, watch YouTube cat videos ... whatever does it for you.

How to make stress your friend

Does this story sound familiar?

It's 8.52 am on a clear, crisp morning. The sun warms 120 students who stand outside the entrance of the gymnasium, waiting. In their hands are clear plastic sleeves containing ballpoint pens, pencils, erasers and pencil sharpeners, their student ID cards and a bottle of water. The air is filled with nervous chatter and the occasional giggle. Our biology exam is due to start in eight minutes and most of us feel stressed.

'Did you study?' I ask Steph.

'Hardly, I was too busy studying for calculus,' she replies.

Next to her, Andrew and Chris stand with two other students, discussing symbiosis.

'No, it's commensalistic,' argues one of the other two students.

'No, it's amensalism,' responds the other.

'I feel sick,' a tall girl complains to Steph.

The exam adjudicator opens the entrance door. At once, a hush runs through the group. Muscles are tensing, hearts are beating faster, we are all breathing harder.

'Good luck,' I hear whispered among the group.

Exams are a stressful time of the year for a lot of students, but the fight-or-flight response that kicks in just before you go into an exam can actually help you perform better. You don't necessarily want to get rid of the stress; you just want to be able to manage your stress so you can use it to your advantage.

When the fight-or-flight response kicks in, your body releases a hormone called oxytocin. You might have heard of this hormone as the 'cuddle hormone'. It makes you crave physical contact with your friends and family. This hormone makes you want to reach out and connect with those around you. This is why you feel so driven to talk to other students about the impending exam before you enter the examination room.

Remember, stress is a physiological response. You can use the fight-or-flight response to your advantage. While you can't control external stress (such as exams) you can control your internal stress and how much inflammation is in your body by making healthy lifestyle choices.

You've got this!

Answer these questions to revise what you've learned about stress management.

1. Can you think of a time when your body had a 'fight-or-flight' reaction? What triggered it?

   _____

   _____

2. Do you think the fight-or-flight response can actually be a good thing? In what situation would this be the case?

   _____

   _____

3. How do you think you would start to feel if your body was in fight-or-flight mode all the time?

   _____

   _____

   Have you ever felt like this before? If so, when and why did you feel this way?

   _____

   _____

4. External stressors are situations you can't avoid, such as exams or personal issues. What are some of the things that have happened in your life that have made you feel stressed?

   _____

   _____

5. Internal stress happens inside your body and causes inflammation. How high/low do you think your levels of internal stress are? Why is this?

_____

_____

6. Have you ever experienced, or are you currently experiencing, chronic stress?

☐ Yes ☐ No

   a. If you answered yes, why do you think this is?

   _____

   _____

   _____

   b. Chronic stress can have serious effects on your physical and psychological health. If you answered yes, can you pinpoint how chronic stress is affecting you?

   _____

   _____

   _____

7. What lifestyle changes could you make to lower your levels of internal stress?

_____

_____

8. What are some hobbies/activities/actions that help you manage/combat stress?

_____

_____

chapter 5

Positive mental health and wellbeing

To be the best person you can be, you need to be healthy in *all* areas of your life.

Think about the dashboard on your/your family's car. There's a range of gauges, including temperature, oil pressure, charging system and fuel. When one meter starts redlining, all of the other gauges are affected. It's a warning sign.

| Physical | Mental | Relational | Spiritual | Emotional |

The five health gauges

The same principle can be applied to your health. If one area of your health begins to suffer, it affects all of the other areas. Living a balanced life means paying attention to all aspects of your health. Most people understand how to be physically healthy. But not everyone knows how to be mentally healthy.

What is positive mental health?

The World Health Organization (WHO) defines positive mental health as:

A state of well-being where individuals are able to: realise their own potential, work productively, cope with the normal stresses of life and make a positive contribution to the community.

Beyond Blue's Be You Mental Health Continuum

Like your physical health, your mental health isn't something that stays the same all the time. Your mental health changes over time in response to internal and external stress.

That's why mental health can be measured across a scale. You may have heard of Beyond Blue. They use a mental health continuum to assess mental health. On the left-hand side of the continuum, your mental health is 'flourishing'. On the right-hand side, your mental health is 'severely impacting everyday activities'.

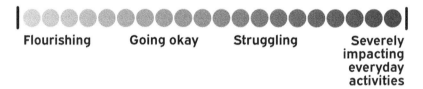

| Flourishing | Going okay | Struggling | Severely impacting everyday activities |

Beyond Blue's Be You Mental Health Continuum

Me

In high school, I struggled with my mental health. At the start of Year 8, my mental health was somewhere towards the middle-to-right part of the mental health continuum (struggling). By the time I reached Year 10, it had moved to the extreme right (severely impacting everyday activities).

Now, my mental health is towards the left-hand end of the scale (flourishing). I feel good about who I am, I have healthy relationships, I enjoy my work and I like to think I contribute towards society in a lot of different positive ways.

You

There are different factors determining where your mental health usually sits on the mental health continuum. Similarly, there are lots of different reasons why your mental health might be at a different place on the continuum right now.

For example, you saw in chapter 4 how internal and external stress can affect how you're thinking, feeling and behaving. Even if you're usually mentally healthy and your mental health sits towards the left-hand side of the continuum, you might find your mental health moving towards the right during times of acute or chronic stress.

Where do you think your mental health is sitting on the mental health continuum right now?

What does it mean to be mentally healthy?

If you are mentally healthy, your mental health sits towards the left-hand side of the mental health continuum. Generally, you feel good. You're able to function well at school and at home. You can cope with stress. You can set yourself personal goals and achieve them. You also contribute towards society in a positive way.

WHAT IS A MENTAL HEALTH ISSUE?

Having a mental health issue means you're experiencing a health problem that affects how you think, feel and behave. Having a mental health issue isn't something to be ashamed of. It's very real and very normal. If you're experiencing a mental health issue, your mental health might be somewhere between the middle part of the scale and the right-hand side of the scale.

WHAT IS A MENTAL ILLNESS?

Having a mental illness means you have a mental health issue that has been diagnosed by a medical practitioner using standardised criteria.

Just like physical illness, mental illness is normal. In fact, every year one in five Australians experience mental illness, 75 per cent of them before they turn 25. NBA player DeMar DeRozan is open about his struggle with depression. He says:

> It's not nothing I'm against or ashamed of. Now, at my age, I understand how many people go through it. Even if somebody can look at it like, 'He goes through it and he's still out there being successful and doing this,' I'm OK with that.

Just like physical illness, there are many different mental illnesses. If you are experiencing and struggling with a mental illness, your mental health will be towards the right-hand side of the mental health continuum.

WHY DOES MENTAL ILLNESS HAPPEN?

Some people are predisposed to developing a certain mental illness. This means their genes, hormones or chemistry make them more likely than others to develop a specific illness. However, the same factors that influence your physical health also influence your mental health. This is why we need to remove the stigma around talking about our mental health. It's the same as physical health. Just because you can't see mental health doesn't make it any less real.

To understand this, think about something you are always prone to getting. For example, I always hurt my back. I also used to get allergies. My wife, Cherith, never hurts her back, but she used to get a lot of colds and suffer from allergies. Some of the reasons you might be prone to getting something are unavoidable (for example, a combination of your genes and other biological factors, or an external stressor such as a relationship breakdown). Some of the reasons you might be prone to developing a particular malady come down to factors you can change, such as:

- negative thought patterns
- low self-esteem
- chronic or acute stress
- use of alcohol, drugs and other substances
- lifestyle factors such as diet, exercise and sleep habits.

When I look back on my experiences growing up, I think I could have avoided my mental health struggles if I'd had the right tools to manage my thoughts and emotions.

My story

In primary school, before Mum moved out, I used to get to go and stay at Oma and Opa's house every weekend. It was just me. My brother was a bit older and wanted to stay home. I loved weekends at Oma and Opa's. Opa hadn't yet developed Parkinson's. He was still independent and did his own thing. It meant I had Oma all to myself.

After school on Fridays, Oma and I would go to the video shop (there wasn't streaming back then). I used to spend ages browsing the aisles and choosing 10 movies to last me all weekend.

Or, on Saturday mornings, over a cooked breakfast, Oma and I would scour the newspaper for cinema movie times. Oma always let me pick what movie we'd go and see. It was awesome—she let me choose any movie I wanted. I remember being so excited to see a movie called The People Under the Stairs. Technically, I was too young to see it. But not with Oma!

(continued)

My coping mechanisms

As time went by, I gradually stopped going to Oma and Opa's on the weekend. I was getting a bit older and I felt like I didn't need a 'babysitter' anymore. But I continued to watch movies at every opportunity.

At school, I was getting bullied relentlessly. At home, my parents' fighting was getting worse. It felt like everyone hated me. I was really lonely. Escaping into the make-believe world of a movie became a way for me to cope with life. When I put on a movie, I felt every muscle in my body relax as the tension released. I didn't know it at the time, but when I watched a movie, I finally stopped being in fight-or-flight mode. My heart rate slowed down. My brain dialled down a few notches. It was a relief to 'zone out' and become absorbed in the story.

Watching movies made me feel better, so I started watching more. I spent more time at the video shop. Eventually, the manager offered me a job.

I enjoyed working at the video shop. My manager was really pretty. She was also nice to me, and we shared snacks during our shifts. At a time when the bullying was getting worse, having someone be kind made me feel less lonely. Having responsibilities and earning my own money also helped boost my dwindling self-esteem.

Internet was dial-up back then, on a 28.8 kbps modem. (Google it: you'll laugh at how slow that was—for example, it took a few minutes for a webpage to load!). I couldn't download movies, so I relied on the video shop for my movie fix. I quickly realised I could sneak movies into my backpack without anyone noticing. I 'borrowed' every horror movie ever made (after that, I couldn't stand in a dark room alone even at the age of 25).

Before long, I'd watched all the horror movies, so I started raiding the pornography section.

At the time, I didn't know how damaging pornography was. I didn't know I could become addicted.

THE DOPAMINE RESPONSE

What is the dopamine response?

Put simply, when you do something you enjoy, your brain releases a surge of a chemical called dopamine. Dopamine is a neurotransmitter that's sent to your brain's reward centre. This is a cluster of cells that lie under your cerebral cortex. Your cerebral cortex is your brain's information processing centre. Some of its functions include motivation, memory and learning.

Dopamine interacts with another neurotransmitter called glutamate. When dopamine and glutamate interact, they take over a system in your brain responsible for reward-related learning. This means your brain learns that a particular behaviour results in a pleasurable outcome.

When you repeatedly expose your brain to a trigger that activates the dopamine response, your cerebral cortex learns to develop a drive for the triggering behaviour or substance. You start craving this behaviour/substance.

Over time, your brain begins to develop a tolerance. If the trigger is a behaviour, you'll feel driven to more extreme versions of that behaviour. If it's a substance, you'll need more of it to achieve the same dopamine response. Behaviours or substances that trigger a strong dopamine response may cause addiction.

My story, continued …

Throughout years 8 and 9, my mental health started deteriorating. I had chronic stress. My body was always in fight-or-flight mode. I couldn't concentrate and I struggled to learn or remember anything. My grades were sliding, and everything felt out of my control.

My home life

As I mentioned earlier, Mum and Dad split up when I was in Year 8 and Mum moved out. My brother had just graduated, and he was *never* at home. Dad started working really long hours and I hardly ever saw him. I knew my dad loved me — I could sense it, which was really important. I also really loved the time we did get to spend together (and I do now, more than ever). We had so much fun making cheese toasties (or 'Brevilles' as they were known in our household — named after the machine). We also had so much fun getting tomato soup ready for dinner on Sunday nights — such a random memory, I know!

The time with him was infrequent though, and when Mum and Dad split up, Dad had to start working longer hours. I hardly ever saw him, which meant we never really talked, and we became strangers to each other. I don't blame Dad at all. I have nothing but the deepest affection for him. At the time I was really hurting, Oma fortunately stepped in. As I mentioned in chapter 1, she used to come over in the mornings and help me get ready for school. She also came over after school to cook dinner for me (and she'd put a plate of food in the fridge for Dad). But she had to be home by 6 pm to help Opa with his dinner. I felt lonely and it took a huge toll on my psychological health.

My school life

During years 8 and 9, the bullying kept getting worse. By the time I reached Year 10, 58 out of 95 guys in my year were either bullying me or watching me get bullied and doing nothing.

Apart from the one time I confided in Dad, I didn't tell anyone about the bullying. I tried to cope with it all on my own.

My descent into pornography addiction

I kept 'borrowing' X-rated videos from the video shop. Pornography triggered a stronger dopamine response in my brain than movies and gaming. It gave me physical pleasure and it also made me feel emotionally numb. When I was feeling really low, watching pornography and masturbating was the only thing that dulled the emotional pain.

Due to the dopamine response, my brain started developing a tolerance to pornography. I needed to start watching more extreme scenes to get the same effect from it. I started developing an addiction. I woke up craving a pornography 'fix'. I stayed up until the early hours of the morning watching pornography and movies, and gaming. I was always wired and tired.

There was no-one there to stop me. And I didn't know how to stop myself.

What happened next?

I became mentally unwell.

I started feeling really anxious all the time. At school, I'd sit in class and stare blankly at the whiteboard. I felt disconnected from my body, as though I was watching myself from up above.

I felt really depressed too. I was filled with a sense of despair. It literally felt as though pain was leaking out from inside me. Time seemed to drag. Every day felt like a month and a month felt like a year.

Sometimes, when the emotional pain became too much to cope with, I'd punch something really hard. I broke gaming controllers and a PC. I punched holes in doors and walls. The physical pain distracted me from the emotional pain for a little

(continued)

while. But inevitably the overwhelming feelings of anxiety and depression would return.

I reached the point where I made a plan to end my life. But I couldn't go through with it. I cared too much about my family. Especially my oma. I didn't want to hurt her. Plus, I hated pain (my dad used to say I was 'allergic' to it).

It was obvious I wasn't coping. I know I looked sick. But not once did anyone reach out to me and say, 'Are you okay?'

MY REASON FOR STARTING ARMED FOR LIFE

The experiences I went through during those school years are one of the main reasons why I started Armed For Life. I wanted other students to know they don't have to go through the emotional pain and anguish I went through. There are things you can do if you're struggling with your mental health.

Try this
Mental health quiz

You might look at the Beyond Blue mental health continuum and know straight away where your mental health is sitting. Or you might feel like you have no idea.

It's normal to feel down from time to time. It's also normal to worry. But if you answer 'yes' to any of the following questions, you might be sitting towards the right-hand side of the continuum.

1. Do you feel really worried or anxious most of the time?

2. Do you feel sad or down most of the time?

3. Are you having trouble concentrating?

4. Are you having extreme mood swings or feeling like you have out-of-control emotional outbursts, such as outbursts of anger?

5. Are you feeling really tired, low in energy or having trouble sleeping?

6. Have you withdrawn from your friends and activities you used to like doing?

7. Are you regularly drinking alcohol or taking drugs?

8. Have your eating habits changed?

9. Are you finding it really difficult to cope with stress?

10. Have you noticed it's harder to relate to people around you and you're feeling disconnected?

11. Are you acting differently from usual?

12. Have you had suicidal thoughts?

If you are experiencing any of the signs above, don't feel discouraged. As I mentioned, there are things you can do to improve your mental health. *You can get better.*

How can you improve your mental health?

In chapter 4, we looked at how to cope with stress in a healthy way. The same strategies apply to improving your mental health. Flick back to that chapter and re-read the section called 'Healthy ways to manage stress', starting on page 92.

Asking for help with a mental health issue

What should you do if you think you're struggling with a mental health issue? If you're struggling with anything, you should always reach out and ask for help. Remember, it might not work the first time. You might need to try three, four or 100 times before you receive the help you need. *Don't give up.*

WHAT SHOULD YOU DO IF YOU FEEL LIKE HARMING YOURSELF?

Sometimes, you might feel more pain than you think you can cope with. If this happens, *you need to reach out and ask for immediate help.* You can:

- call Beyond Blue on 1300 224 636

- call Lifeline on 13 11 14

- call the Kids Helpline on 1800 55 1800.

If your life is in immediate danger:

- call 000

- go to the emergency department of a hospital.

My story

Several years ago, I went through a really dark period. My previous marriage fell apart and the stress of it led me to have a mental breakdown. Prior to my separation, I was feeling mentally healthy. After my ex-wife and I separated, I started feeling really low. I couldn't sleep and it was a struggle to get out of bed in the mornings. I couldn't eat and I lost 8 kilograms in two weeks. It was the lowest I've felt since I was in Year 10.

I fell into such a dark place that I couldn't see a way out. But I knew I needed to change how I was thinking and behaving or I wasn't going to survive. I decided to make just one small change.

I started scheduling my time.

This behaviour made it easier for me to make a second change, which led to a third change, and so forth. Once I started to see light at the end of the tunnel, I thought I could start walking towards it.

Gradually, the pain started to get a bit better. It didn't happen overnight, but eventually, I started feeling better. My mental health began to shift towards the healthy end of the mental health continuum.

How I recovered from my mental illness

As you read in the story above, I started making small changes to slowly get myself out of the dark hole I fell into after my divorce. Here are some of the changes I made. They're all invaluable tools for coping with and recovering from mental illness.

TIME MANAGEMENT

When I was feeling depressed, time seemed to really drag. The days felt endless. I decided to start splitting my day into three time slots. That way, I only had to focus on making it through to the end of one time slot before focusing on the next. My time slots were:

- from when I woke up until 12 noon

- from 12 noon until 6 pm

- from 6 pm until bedtime (which was usually pretty late because I couldn't sleep).

I lived alone, so it was easy to stay in bed and avoid people. To overcome this, I made it my goal to make sure I was out and spending time with at least one other person during one time slot each day. In the other two time periods, I promised myself I had to be in contact with at least one other person. Even if it was just via a text message.

I was lucky to have a handful of really close friends to rely on during this period. Being able to reach out and talk to my friends made it easier to process my emotional pain and grief.

PRAYER

I know not everyone is religious and I don't expect anyone else to have the same beliefs I do. But I've been a Christian since I was 18 years old and turning to prayer was the one thing that helped me most during this period. I prayed every day. Sometimes, I prayed for an hour or two at a time. I couldn't focus on work, or anything else for that matter. It felt as though my life was falling apart, so I prayed just to get through the day. My faith and relationship with Jesus kept me going during this time.

EXERCISE

I was really purposeful about going to the gym. I knew my body needed the endorphins and serotonin to help me feel better. Sometimes, just the thought of getting dressed and leaving the house felt impossible. But I made sure I showed up to the gym every single day. Even if it wasn't a productive gym session, the goal was just to show up no matter how depressed, sick or tired I was feeling.

NUTRITION

The separation from my ex-wife was hugely stressful. It made me feel sick all the time. My digestive system started struggling and I started feeling really bloated. So I began to change what I ate. I didn't give my diet a complete overhaul. Instead, I started trying to make better choices with each meal.

TALKING TO A PROFESSIONAL

I'd seen a counsellor in the past, but I felt like it hadn't really helped me. We hadn't clicked. I decided to try again and I started seeing a psychologist. From the outset, I felt as though he understood me. He helped me to identify my issues and take responsibility for them.

Eventually, things started to come together for me. My mental health started moving towards the left on the mental health continuum. I felt the anxiety lessen. My mood began to improve. It took a long time to fully recover from the stress and trauma of my relationship breakdown. But on reflection, I needed it to happen the way it did. I needed to learn how to own up to my problems and take responsibility for my actions. In the long run, talking to a therapist helped me take ownership of my mistakes and the unhealthy behaviours that contributed to my relationship breaking down. Now, I'm much healthier for it.

Why do you need to be mentally healthy to be resilient?

If you're struggling with your mental health, remember that it's nothing to be ashamed about. There are things you can do to improve your mental health. It's not something you need to suffer in silence. It's also really important to see a professional and talk about what's going on for you. We all have problems; no-one is immune to mental illness, just as no-one is immune to catching the flu (regardless of whether you get the flu jab or not).

Being mentally healthy is essential for resilience. Why? If you're mentally healthy, your mental health gauge is 'topped up'.

What does this mean?

You'll be able to think clearly and objectively. Because you'll be feeling healthy, you won't base your decisions around trying to 'feel better'. Rather, you'll be able to think through problems and respond in a positive way. When issues do crop up, you'll feel armed to tackle them with ease. Finally, you'll feel confident with your decisions and the way you're managing life.

Being as mentally healthy as you can is an awesome place to be in (I know because I've been on both ends of the mental health continuum). Aim to get your mental health as 'flourishing' as possible by managing your stress, working on your self-esteem, being self-aware and making healthy lifestyle choices. You won't regret it.

You've got this!

Answer these questions to revise what you've learned about mental health and wellbeing.

1. Mental health isn't something that's fixed; it's something you can work on improving. Identify where you think your mental health currently sits on Beyond Blue's Be You Mental Health Continuum.

Flourishing   **Going okay**   **Struggling**   **Severely impacting everyday activities**

Why did you mark yourself in this particular circle?

_____

_____

2. Can you identify someone you could talk to about your mental health?

_____

_____

3. How does your mental health affect your self-esteem?

_____

_____

4. How does your mental health affect how resilient you are?

_____

_____

5. Have any of your friends ever experienced depression or anxiety or another mental health condition? How do you think you can best support them?

_____

_____

6. Do you think there's a connection between bullying and mental health? If so, what is it?

_____

_____

7. Your mental health affects your physical health, and your physical health affects your mental health. List some of the ways your own mental health is affected by your physical health and vice versa.

_____

_____

_____

_____

8. RUOK Day is a day that aims to inspire and empower us to reach out to people around us. That way, we can have a conversation with someone who might be struggling with their mental health. Can you think of someone you can check in with today by asking, 'Are you okay?'

_____

_____

chapter 6

Self-awareness and managing emotions

Eight, nine, ten!

Stepping forward, I release the barbell onto the rack and exhale. My heart is thumping. I'm caked in sweat. I don't lift heavy because I'm prone to injury and I've never been interested in maxing out. Plus, I usually train on my own. This means I don't have a 'spotter' to help me if I overestimate what I'm capable of lifting. But I still train hard. When my heart is pounding and I'm out of breath and I know I'm at 80 per cent, I always push through for two more reps. The mental challenge makes me feel more resilient in everyday life.

Stepping back and leaning on the barbell for support, I stop for two minutes to rest and catch my breath. I spot my reflection in the long floor-to-ceiling mirrors. My face is flushed, and my muscles are inflamed (but this is a good type of inflammation). I feel satisfied with what I see.

In the mirror, I see two guys I recognise training at a bench further along the room. One is the owner of the gym. He recently won Strongman (a weightlifting competition). Both guys lift really heavy – at least three times what I lift. The gym owner is chatting to his training partner while he racks his weights. I look away and when I turn back, the two guys start laughing.

They're laughing at me, I think. It's an automatic negative thought (ANT) though, surely? There's no way they're laughing at me. They're not even looking in my direction. *Focus*, I think to myself. *Rest time is up. Get back on the bar.* I step forward, lift the bar and start another round. My mind zones out.

I still get ANTs all the time. It usually happens if I think I'm being excluded. Or if I think someone's making fun of me. It stems back to when I used to get bullied in high school. I remember how, in class, the teacher would say 'Find a partner' but I'd have no-one. Or when I'd be sitting on my own at recess or lunch and students standing in tight little huddles would look over at me and laugh.

I'm out of school now, and I've grown up a lot. I have a healthy self-esteem and there's no reason for anyone to bully me. But I still get paranoid about it. I know I need to be aware of negative thoughts and catch them when they happen.

Self-awareness and ANTs

There might be ongoing ANTs that plague you. They might be a throwback to a stressful situation. Or maybe someone made a negative comment about you, and it stuck with you.

Everyone has hang-ups. Everyone has ANTs. You might look at someone and think, *They've got it together.* It might be because they're popular at school. They might be considered really good looking or pretty or wear cool clothes. Or they might be book smart and receive top marks in everything. I promise you: this person has ANTs too. It's human nature. You can't escape negative thinking. The trick is to be aware of negative thoughts, catch them when they happen and immediately reframe them into something more positive.

What do ANTs have to do with emotions?

If you're aware of your negative thoughts, it's easier to know why you're feeling a certain way. If you're not paying attention to your thoughts, strong emotions can seem to come out of nowhere. They can make you feel moody for no reason.

The three negative categories of emotion

All emotions are valid. It's so important to give your emotions a space to exist. Emotions are biological in nature and it's beneficial for you to experience them. Why?

- They motivate you to do something.
- They help you avoid dangerous situations.
- They guide you in making decisions.
- They help you relate to other people.

There are four big categories of emotion: bad, sad, mad and glad. Three of these emotions are negative (bad, sad and mad). It's normal to want to avoid these emotions because they don't feel very nice.

Me

Personally, I used to struggle with all three negative emotions in a big way. I used to wake up in the mornings feeling sick with dread. I didn't understand why I was feeling so awful, so I just tried to push the emotions away. I also felt really low. I didn't want anyone to know how depressed I was feeling. In part, I felt ashamed, and in part, I felt like I deserved to feel this way. I was experiencing a lot of anger, but I didn't know how to manage it,

(continued)

so I just tried to push it 'down'. Every time something happened to make me angry, I'd suppress the feelings just to try and cope. Eventually, the angry feelings would build up and I'd explode. I'd 'die' in a game, and suddenly I'd be filled with blinding rage and I'd smash my Xbox controller. I felt completely out of control. This happened eight times (I also punched a PC and kicked a hole through the wall), but still I didn't realise that I was out of control because I wasn't dealing with my emotions.

You

Do you find yourself getting stuck in feelings of anxiety, depression or anger for no real reason? It's normal to feel moody—especially in your teenage years—but if you become trapped in these emotions, it's a red flag.

FEELING BAD

When you feel bad, you tend to feel anxious. You might recognise it as feeling 'yucky' or 'gross'. The first thing you might want to do when anxious feelings hit is reject them.

FEELING SAD

Feeling sad can range from feeling slightly down to feeling really depressed and hopeless. It's normal to try and hide these feelings because you don't want to feel depressed or for other people to see you feeling this way.

FEELING MAD

Feeling mad ranges from mild irritation or annoyance to experiencing uncontrollable rage. You might want to push down feelings of anger. It doesn't feel good, and suppressing it gives you temporary relief. The problem with pushing down your anger is it builds up and up until you lose control.

Managing your emotions

How should you manage the three negative emotions in a healthy way? Instead of getting stuck in an emotion, you can choose to take control of it by recognising, processing and expressing the emotion. Let's look at each of these three tools for helping you manage your emotions.

Recognise the emotion

Recognising an emotion is a process known as self-awareness. I've already spoken about how self-awareness is the practice of being aware of your emotions and how they affect you. An important part of recognising an emotion is being able to name it. For example, if you're feeling anxious, say to yourself *I'm feeling anxious.* (Note: don't say, *I am anxious.* It's a feeling – it's not who you are.) If you recognise the emotion you're feeling, you can start to process it.

Process the emotion

Processing an emotion is where the role of the personal detective comes into play. It's about mentally working through any negative emotions you're experiencing. Ask yourself:

- What category am I feeling: mad, sad, bad?
- What problem or issue caused these feelings?
- Are any ANTs contributing to this issue?

Being pro-active is about asking yourself *Why am I feeling [insert emotion]?* It doesn't need to be a single process. It can be an ongoing practice. For example, I know I need to be aware of managing my anger. I'm better at it than I used to be, but I'm still not perfect. I've learned that when I become angry, I need to remove myself from the situation and process the emotion first.

For example, when Cherith and I fight (all couples have healthy conflict, it's normal – we'll look at this in chapter 10), I know I'm prone to reacting by lashing out. It's normal to react with anger if you feel emotional hurt or pain. When this happens, I try to step away and think things through. *Why am I feeling so angry?* I don't always do this – I still mess up from time to time – but I'm better than I used to be.

Express the emotion

It's healthy to express negative emotions instead of rejecting, hiding or suppressing them. Once you've mentally worked through an emotion, it's important to 'unleash' the feeling in a productive way. This may involve creative expression (writing and journaling), exercise (resistance training or going for a run), talking to someone about your feelings or addressing the person who upset you.

Managing emotions and resilience

Managing your emotions is closely tied to resilience because when you respond to feelings, instead of reacting to them, you're better able to cope with challenges. When you recognise, process and express your emotions, you're in a better position to look at yourself objectively. This means you can look at yourself with an open mind. You consider the facts, instead of relying on your personal judgements and feelings.

Review your emotional processing

Do you remember how, in chapter 2, we looked at the three stages of resilience? The third stage, 'Review', involves using self-reflection to look at how you dealt with a problem. You can use this process to look at how you managed a negative emotion too:

- Did you recognise the emotion?
- Did you mentally think through why you're experiencing the negative emotion?

- Did you express your emotion in a healthy way, or did you do what made you feel better?

If you're feeling stuck in an emotion, think about why you're stuck. Are you recognising the emotion for what it is? Do you need to work on processing the emotion? Or do you need to find a way to express the emotion?

The more often you practise the review process, the more resilient you'll become.

Developing self-awareness

An important part of self-awareness is understanding yourself: your personality, character, strengths and weaknesses. When you develop a deep knowledge about who you are, it's easier to deal with a problem, trauma or crisis. Start by thinking: *What are some of the things I love doing?*

Me

I love going to the movies. I recently took my son Cale. As we stepped into the foyer, I could hear a hum of excitement as kids, teenagers and adults all stood around in groups, laughing and chatting. As soon as we joined the line for tickets, I felt my heartbeat quicken in anticipation. It reminded me of being a kid and going to the movies with Oma.

The smell of warm, buttery popcorn hit me and, suddenly, I was starving. Thinking about the popcorn made me thirsty too. Then I started thinking about the enormous soft drinks you get at the candy bar. 'Hey, wait up mate!', I yelled at Cale. We'd bought our tickets and he was already headed towards

(continued)

the snacks. Cale turned around, hands on his hips. 'Hurry up, Dad!' he shouted.

Armed with our popcorn combos, Cale and I headed for the dark, cave-like theatre. Cale bounded up the stairs, finding us seats. Plonking myself down, I literally felt the tension melt from my muscles. The cinema is my place to chill and just 'be'. It's also a place where I can connect and have fun with Cale. The time we get to spend getting lost in the FX, feeling the boom of the atmos in our chests. Then we get emotionally caught up in the story: laughing and crying (yes – I'm a crier at the movies).

I also love going to the movies on a date night with my beautiful wife, Cherith. This photo is of us in Bali in 2019 celebrating our first anniversary. Last time, we went out for burgers before heading to an art-house cinema in Leederville (one of the cool, hipster inner-city suburbs of Perth). Sometimes, we just hang out at home together and watch a movie in our theatre room.

Loving movies is a huge part of who I am. Through watching movies, I've learned I'm a really sensitive guy and I love soppy, romantic movies and tear-jerkers. This discovery has been part of my self-awareness journey.

My story

Developing self-awareness takes practice. It's something that took me a really long time. During school, all I wanted was to be liked. As the bullying got worse, I tried harder to fit in. I pretended to be strong and tough, but deep down I knew I was gentle and sensitive.

Instead of valuing the person I was, I tried to become someone I wasn't. I didn't respect myself enough to take the time to understand my likes and dislikes, what I loved or what made me tick. Instead, I tried to prescribe myself personal qualities based on what was 'cool' or what would make me fit in at school. I'm sure everyone could see straight through me and as a result, I had hardly any friends.

When I turned 18, I reached a turning point. I only just scraped through and graduated Year 12, but my grades weren't good enough to get into uni. I didn't know myself and I wasn't sure what I wanted to do with my life. I didn't have a strong support network of friends or family to lean on for guidance. I felt lost, alone and aimless.

Gradually, I came to the realisation that I needed to start being real with myself. Depending on other people for a sense of self-worth was getting me nowhere. I needed to take ownership of my life and start moving forwards. I started by getting a job volunteering as a speaker for an organisation that went into schools. It was also around this time that I chose to start valuing my life. I chose to develop a faith and I became a Christian.

I didn't become self-aware overnight. It took years of trying to learn about who I was and who I wanted to become. But when I decided to be real and listen to my problems, things started to improve for me. Over time, I realised being sensitive isn't a bad thing. It means I'm a good listener. I like helping people with their problems. This is what led me on the path to starting Armed For Life.

You

Your teenage years are all about learning who you are. As you start becoming aware of yourself—your likes, dislikes, needs and desires—be confident in that person. Never reject or silence parts of yourself you don't like. Learn to accept *all* of yourself (warts and all).

How to become self-aware

Becoming self-aware isn't something you can do instantly. It's a gradual process of learning to recognise and process your thoughts, feelings and emotions. It took me a long time to start understanding why I was thinking the way I was. It's about building new neural pathways and beginning to let go of some of the redundant ones. Some tools you can use to start becoming self-aware are:

- practise mindfulness
- record your thoughts
- set SMART goals and review them
- be honest with yourself.

All of these ways of achieving self-awareness are linked. Self-awareness is about holistic introspection. That is, looking inwards at your whole self, accepting your whole self and being completely honest with yourself. Here's how to get started.

Practise mindfulness

Practising mindfulness is about bringing your attention to the present moment. The two ways you can achieve this are by focusing on the *now* and by being purposeful about existing in the present time and space. How do you achieve this?

PAY ATTENTION TO YOUR SURROUNDINGS

Practise mindfulness by paying attention to your five senses: what do you hear, see, smell, feel and taste? This exercise will help bring your focus into the now.

TRY TO LIVE 'IN THE MOMENT'

Be proactive about activities that help bring you into the moment.

Everyone is different. Here's a list of ideas of ways to achieve mindfulness:

- yoga
- breathing exercises
- Pilates
- tai chi
- meditation
- prayer
- going into nature
- creative expression (e.g. painting, dancing).

Reach out to me on social (@armedforlife) with your mindfulness practices.

Record your thoughts

Your thoughts matter. Writing your thoughts down can help give you clarity on situations. It can help you think objectively and become aware of any subconscious or unconscious emotions you're experiencing.

One form of journaling, called 'stream of consciousness', involves putting pen to paper (or fingers to keyboard) and writing/typing whatever comes to mind. This method can help you become aware of what you're feeling, and what triggers certain feelings.

Journaling can also improve your self-esteem. It's a space for self-discovery where you can find what makes *you* happy. Not sure how to get started? Pull out a notepad and answer the question, 'How did you feel today?'

Set SMART goals and review them

There are all sorts of personal goals in life. The purpose of setting personal goals is self-improvement. Someone you know might have goals around fitness or sporting achievements, while another person might set personal goals around achieving certain grades or getting into a course of study after graduating high school.

Goal setting is an opportunity to map out where you want to go in life, and the steps you need to take to get there. When you track the progress of your goals, you can look at yourself objectively to check whether the decisions you're making day to day align with your big-picture goals.

Not sure how to set your goals? Start with a bucket list: create a list of all the things you want in life. Choose one item from your bucket list and think of how you can achieve it. Create a goal that is 'SMART' (a concept coined by George T. Doran in 1981).

The SMART method of setting goals is a terrific tool to use when setting your goals. SMART stands for:

- S: specific
- M: measurable
- A: attainable
- R: relevant
- T: time-bound.

SPECIFIC GOALS

When setting your goal, think about the five 'Ws':

- *Who* needs to be involved to help you achieve your goal?
- *What* exactly do you want to achieve?
- *When* do you want to achieve your goal by?
- *Where* is your goal going to be achieved? (if there's a special location or event)
- *Why* do you want to achieve your goal?

MEASURABLE GOALS

Think about a way you can measure the progress of your goal. For example, if you want to improve your self-esteem, your goal might involve identifying five negative thoughts per day and reframing these thoughts into something more positive.

ATTAINABLE GOALS

Make sure your goal is something you can actually achieve. Be honest with yourself. If your goal is too ambitious, tone it down a notch. For example, I spent years trying to set myself the goal of playing A-grade basketball, when – in reality – I was too anxious to even try out for the team. I should have made my goal to try out. That way, I would have been more likely to achieve it.

RELEVANT GOALS

Look at the goal you have written down. Does it make sense when it comes to your bigger goals and dreams in life? For example, I make goals around my personal fitness that help me improve my skills on the basketball court.

TIME-BOUND GOALS

Make sure your goal has a due date. You can set a goal, but if it lacks a realistic deadline, then chances are you won't succeed. A good rule of thumb is that it takes 21 days to create/break a habit. If you're setting a goal around creating/changing your lifestyle, ensure it has at least 21 days to establish, but not so long that it's open-ended.

Examples of SMART goals

These are some examples of goals that use the SMART goal-setting method:

- A personal goal about improving self-image:

  My goal is to pay attention to ANTs every time I see my reflection (at least once in the morning and once at night when I'm getting ready for the day/for bed) and, if I catch one, reframe it into something more positive. I'll write the ANT and its replacement in my journal each night for the whole of April and during the first week of May, I'll take notice of the thoughts I have when I see my reflection in the mirror. I'll then look at my journal for April and assess whether my ANTs about seeing my reflection have improved.

- A personal goal about being more self-aware:

  I know I drink too much alcohol when I'm feeling stressed, low or anxious. For the next seven days, each time I find myself wanting to drink, I'll stop and write a list in my phone of what I'm thinking and feeling. At the end of the week (on Sunday), I'll look at what ANT triggered me to want to drink most often. Then I'll create a new goal around managing this ANT.

- A personal goal about making healthy friendships:

  My goal is to make a new friend who makes me feel supported and valued. I'll achieve this goal by joining the running club and challenging myself to speak to one new person each time I attend for the next two months. At the end of the two months, I'll see whether I've made a new, healthy friend or whether I need to try something different.

- A personal goal about reaching out for help with bullying:

  My goal is to talk to my PE teacher about the bullying I'm experiencing and how it's affecting me before the end of the week. The outcome I need is for the teacher to help me manage the bullying. If I don't get his support and a plan going forward after I talk to him, I'll try a different teacher.

Be honest with yourself

If you're willing to look at yourself and be completely honest – even if it hurts to do so – you have the opportunity to see your *real* self.

Even if you learn something about yourself that makes you balk, remember to be objective. Accept yourself 100 per cent. Something you thought was a weakness can be reframed into something positive.

How self-awareness makes you more resilient

Self-awareness is introspection, but it's not navel gazing or being self-absorbed. You might act in a certain way and be completely unaware of it. Being self-aware and learning to manage your emotions will help you in all areas of your life.

I've had times in my life where I haven't been self-aware, and it's been really damaging on both myself and the people around me. When I was in my mid thirties, I was in a really unhealthy relationship. There was toxicity on both sides of the relationship. On my side, I wasn't being self-aware, and I wasn't managing my emotions. I was suppressing my anger.

I started seeing a psychologist, who helped me realise how subtly controlling I was being. It was because, deep down, I was scared of losing my ex. The psychologist described it as hundreds of little strings I'd set up to try and ensure my ex wouldn't leave. It was really damaging for both of us.

My psychologist knew I was into movies. During one session, he said to me, 'Gaining self-awareness is like watching a thriller in which the main character has amnesia. But, as he goes through the movie, he begins to realise he's the *bad* guy, not the good guy.'

I got it. I'd been spending my whole life blaming everyone else for my pain and anger. In high school, I blamed the students who were bullying me. I blamed my parents for getting a divorce. Now, in my twenties, I blamed my ex-wife for leaving me. Instead of blaming everyone else for my problems, I needed to look inwards, towards myself, for the real cause. I needed to own up to my problems and review my decision making. At the time, I had an internal crisis. I started thinking *Should I even be doing Armed for Life? What makes me good enough to help other people? Look at how broken I am.*

Then, I decided to forgive myself. I looked at myself objectively and reviewed my decisions. I accepted I'd made some huge mistakes and set some goals for improvement. I'm nowhere near perfect. I'm still a work-in-progress. We all are. But now I know how important it is to be proactive about practising self-awareness and to continually work towards managing negative emotions.

Being self-aware and knowing how to manage your emotions will naturally make you more resilient. When you know why you're experiencing certain feelings, you can identify the thoughts that triggered the feelings. Taking responsibility for your emotions is an empowering position to be in. It's an awesome feeling knowing you'll be able to deal with any negative feelings or emotions that crop up with ease.

You've got this!

Answer these questions to revise what you've learned about self-awareness and managing emotions.

1. Do you ever find yourself getting stuck in feelings?

   ☐ Yes ☐ No

   a. What feelings do you get stuck in (for example, feeling angry or feeling low)?

   _____

   _____

   b. What category of emotion is this feeling: bad, sad, mad or glad?

   _____

2. Why do you think it's important to think *I'm feeling [insert emotion]* instead of *I am [insert emotion]*? For example, why is it important to think *I'm feeling anxious,* instead of *I am anxious*?

   _____

   _____

3. Do you think you are self-aware? Why/why not?

   _____

   _____

4. Practising mindfulness means focusing on the present instead of worrying about the future or ruminating on the past. What are some ways you might draw your attention to being *in the moment*?

   _____

   _____

5. There are lots of different ways of keeping a journal ('journaling'). You don't have to have a notebook stuffed under your mattress or a Tumblr account. Think about apps where you can record just one line a day, or just a single emoji. You could start a private blog, or you might prefer doodling/drawing/sketching or vlogging (video blogging). What type of journaling appeals to you?

_____

6. Effective goals need to be SMART:

S: Specific

M: Measurable

A: Attainable

R: Relevant

T: Time-bound

Have a go at setting a personal goal using the SMART method:

Specific

When setting your goal, think about the five 'Ws' and write down:

- *Who* needs to be involved to help you achieve your goal?

  _____

  _____

- *What* exactly do you want to achieve?

  _____

  _____

- *When* do you want to achieve your goal by?

  _____

  _____

- *Where* is your goal going to be achieved (if there's a special location or event)?

  _____

  _____

- *Why* do you want to achieve your goal?

  _____

  _____

Measurable

Write down a way you can measure the progress of your goal.

For example, if you want to improve your self-esteem, your goal might involve identifying five negative thoughts per day and reframing these thoughts into something more positive.

_____

_____

Attainable

Is your goal something you can actually achieve? Be honest with yourself.

☐ Yes ☐ No

If you answered 'no', what is a way you can tone down your goal by a notch?

_____

_____

Relevant

Look at the goal you have written down. Does it make sense when it comes to your bigger goals and dreams in life?

☐ Yes ☐ No

Time-bound

What is the date you are aiming to achieve your goal by?

_____

7. How can you use self-awareness and manage your emotions to ensure you'll feel okay if something happens to prevent you from achieving your goal?

_____

_____

chapter 7

Healthy friendships

My first experience of having a 'friend' was in Year 1. The kid was Stephen. We were hanging out at recess, hiding in the bushes and building a fort.

'Adam, go get more sticks for the walls,' Stephen ordered and I lumbered off, collecting branches and bringing them back to him.

'We need leafier branches so we can be camouflaged,' I suggested, stepping back to inspect Stephen's work after handing him the pile of sticks.

The bell chimed. Recess was finished. Time to go back to the classroom.

'If you go back, I'm not going to be your friend anymore,' said Stephen. I looked at him, then looked back at the oval. I didn't want Stephen to not want to be my friend anymore. *I'd better stay here,* I thought.

'Okay,' I said, clambering into our half-built fort beside him.

Stephen started inspecting the gaps between the skinny sticks holding up our fort.

'The teachers can see us easy,' he said. 'You need to go and get more leafy branches from over there.'

'You're bossy,' I told him. Stephen pointed to a big branch. It had fallen over onto the oval.

'Don't get caught,' he said. I crawled out of the fort and looked at him.

'Why don't you come with me?' I asked, wondering why I had to take all the risk.

'I need to stay here and guard the fort,' Stephen announced.

'Oh, okay,' I replied. *I guess that makes sense.* I crawled down to the spot he'd pointed to. Then I started picking the leafiest bits.

I got back to base safe and sound and we finished our fort. We covered the rest of the gaps with twigs and dried leaves.

'We'll come back to it at lunch,' Stephen said, wiping his hands on his shorts. I nodded.

'We should probably get back to class before we get caught,' I suggested. It had been about 10 minutes since the bell had rung.

'Okay,' Stephen replied, agreeing to one of my ideas for the first time ever. We pelted for it. Across the oval, running for our lives. When we got to the classroom Stephen hissed 'duck'. We crouched down.

'You go first,' he said. 'I'll keep watch.'

We peered through the open classroom door on our hands and knees. I dashed across the room on all fours. Stephen followed. The other kids looked at us and started laughing.

'Adam! Stephen!' the teacher shouted at us. Uh oh. We were going to get in Big Trouble! 'Go to the principal's office,' the teacher said, pointing at the door.

'Yes Miss,' I replied, standing upright. Stephen stood up behind me.

'It was Adam's fault,' accused Stephen. *It was not! Stephen told me I had to stay. It wasn't my idea!* I turned to him. I was so mad! I didn't want to be his friend anymore.

Stephen and I did get in a lot of trouble from the principal. We got the cane (yes – I'm that old). I remember it hurt so much. I was such a well-behaved student after that.

I stopped playing with Stephen. Although I was only six years old, I knew he wasn't being a good friend. Friends are supposed to stick up for each other. Not try to get each other in trouble. Or blame each other in front of the grown-ups. So I stopped being friends with Stephen and I started playing with some of the other kids at recess and lunch.

The evolution of friendship

Did you know that 'friendship' isn't limited to humans? Most animals have acquaintances, but only a select number of mammals are capable of true friendship. These mammals are higher primates, members of the horse family, elephants, cetaceans (whales, dolphins and porpoises) and camelids (camels, llamas and alpacas).

Social connection and the ability to form friendships is linked to brain size. Remember how, in chapter 2, we spoke about Dunbar's number?

Robin Dunbar came up with this number almost by accident. As a specialist in primate behaviour, Dunbar was working on an unrelated topic, trying to figure out why primates spend so much time on their grooming. He came across a new hypothesis: that the size of an animal's neocortex could predict the group size of that animal (and that primates have big brains because they live in large social groups).

Dunbar decided to apply this idea to humans. He did the maths and calculated that humans can maintain up to about 150 social connections. Dunbar proposed that humans have developed large brains to enable them to live in a large social group.

What's the advantage of living in a big group?

There are clear advantages to animals living in a large social group. Imagine if you were living in the wild. You'd probably feel safer in a group because you're less likely to become victim to a predator. You'd have your groupmates there to help you find food, water and shelter. It's also easier to find a mate if you're already in a group.

It makes sense for animals to form social connections in the wild, but what about humans? Why is it important for us to have people in our lives who we know, like, trust and care about?

Why is friendship important?

Humans are a social species. We are tribal by nature. Wanting to feel as though we 'belong' isn't just a desire. It's in our DNA.

As humans, we have two deeply ingrained needs:

- We need to feel loved.
- We need to feel like we belong.

Having healthy friendships in our lives meets our needs for love and belonging. It makes us more resilient and able to cope with life's ups and downs.

What about that horrible feeling of getting left out?

Did you know your brain responds in the same way to getting left out as it does to physical pain? Social pain and physical pain both activate a region of your brain known as the dorsal anterior cingulate cortex (dACC). That's why it genuinely hurts or 'cuts deep' when you feel excluded by your friends.

You might be familiar with the feeling of looking over at a group of really close friends and longing to be a part of it. If you don't have healthy friendships, it can affect how you feel about yourself. You might start questioning yourself: *Am I even capable of making friends?*

I always felt left out and excluded at school. When I tried to make friends, it felt awkward and 'forced'. I didn't know what to say, so I'd say something stupid or do something equally stupid and then I'd get laughed at (and not in a nice way). In the end, I just gave up trying.

How many friends should you have?

When it comes to friendships, quality is more important than quantity. Personally, I can count the number of close friends I have on one hand.

On the flipside, it's important to have more than just one close friend. Sometimes, I'll go into a school and a student will say to me, 'I have a BFF (best friend for life), so I don't need any other friends'. There's nothing wrong with having a BFF. But you shouldn't *only* have a BFF. How come?

If you only have one close friend, you'll end up needy. You'll put too much pressure on that person. What happens if you have a fight? Or if your BFF makes another friend, or ends up in a relationship?

A NOTE ON SOCIAL MEDIA 'FRIENDS'

Socials play a huge role in the life of almost every teenager I meet, but life isn't about how many friends/followers you have on your social platforms. Getting 'likes' gives you a dopamine hit: it makes you feel good *temporarily*. But it's nothing in comparison to having real, in-person friends who you know, trust and care about.

The benefits of friendship

Friends can be awesome. Apart from helping you survive school, there are many benefits to having healthy friendships. These are:

- better health across all five gauges (physical, mental, emotional, relational and spiritual)
- a sense of belonging
- a boost to your happiness and lowered stress levels
- improved self-esteem and self-confidence
- help for when you're facing challenges or coping with crisis and trauma.

The thing is, you'll only get these benefits from a healthy friendship. An unhealthy or toxic friendship can cause great harm.

Me

I've already mentioned I was fairly well liked at school until Year 4. I was sporty, which automatically made me popular. Then I became overweight. I started getting bullied. My self-esteem plummeted and it became hard to make friends. You'll recall the incident I described in chapter 3 about my four closest 'friends' turning on me during a basketball game. It knocked my confidence badly and I lost trust in the guys who were supposed to be my friends. These turned out not to be healthy friendships.

You

What kinds of friendships do you have? Your friends have a deep impact on who you are now and who you will become. The famous saying goes, 'You are the average of the five people you spend the most time with'.

Think about those in your inner circle. Do they have the qualities of the type of person you would like to become? Are your friends nice, friendly, caring and supportive? Or are they selfish, manipulative and easily angered?

Remember this: if your friends do something with you, they'll also do it to you. If your friends gossip to you about everyone, you can be guaranteed they also gossip about you to other people.

What is a 'healthy friendship'?

What exactly is a 'healthy' friendship? A healthy friendship is made up of two people. This means you need to be self-aware and look at the type of friend *you* are. A quote from one of my favourite philosophers, Ralph Waldo Emerson, goes:

> *The only way to have a friend is to be one.*

Do you ever notice that popular students seem to find it easy to make new friends? That if you don't have many (or any) friends, it's really hard to make new friends?

Generally, if you have high self-esteem, you'll make lots of friends. This will give your self-esteem a healthy boost, and you'll find it even easier to make friends. It's a cycle you can tap into if you use the right approach.

You might need to make new friends if you've changed schools or if you've swapped up your sports/after-school activities. You might feel like you've 'outgrown' friends, or that they've 'outgrown' you.

Or, you might have just distanced yourself from some unhealthy friendships. It's normal as a teenager to find yourself in the situation where you need to make new friends. How do you know what qualities to look for in a healthy friendship?

The qualities of a healthy friendship

It's so important to be sure your friendships are healthy because it can be easy to get involved in an unhealthy friendship without realising it. Here are some tips on what to look for in a healthy friendship.

HEALTHY FRIENDSHIPS ARE REAL AND HONEST

Vulnerability is at the heart of friendship. A friendship isn't healthy if you feel like you need to pretend to be someone you're not. Real connection is based on being your true, awkward self. (Yes, we all have awkward and imperfect bits. Not just physically, but also in our personalities.) Often, the best friendships begin when we find someone else who has a similar weird, awkward or imperfect bit and we connect over it. It's that feeling of 'me too!'

You also shouldn't have to try too hard. I see this all the time in my Armed For Life camps. We run two camps every year. On day one, there's always one person trying really hard to make friends. Trying *too* hard. It works for the first two days. By day three, this person is alone and upset because no-one wants to be their friend. Why? Because they're not being real. Honest friendships are built on connecting over similar interests like music, books, movies ... or maybe you both hate Fortnite?

HEALTHY FRIENDSHIPS ARE ABOUT CARING AND BEING SUPPORTIVE

When you find yourself facing a tough challenge, who sticks around to help? Your true friends aren't only there for you during the good times, they're there for you during the tough times too.

It took me until I reached my thirties to start understanding what a healthy friendship was. Since then, I've worked hard to make friends who are good for me. I mentioned earlier in the book that when my second marriage fell apart, I had a mental breakdown. I started struggling with feeling really depressed and anxious. I felt my mental health sliding downwards by the day, and I felt as though I couldn't pick myself up again.

During this time, I leaned heavily on my inner circle just to be able to survive. I had seven people in my inner circle during this time. Six guys and one girl. As I mentioned in chapter 5, I made sure I stayed in touch with my closest friends every day. Revealing my thoughts and how I was feeling to these friends made me really vulnerable. They could have laughed at me or made fun of how I was feeling. Or they could have started avoiding me. Instead, the friends in my inner circle made it a priority to respond to my text messages. They spent time with me, even when I didn't feel as though I was much fun to be around. I felt supported and cared about.

HEALTHY FRIENDSHIPS ARE ABOUT TRUST

You need to be able to trust your friends. You need to feel confident they won't go behind your back or betray you.

When I turned to my inner circle after my separation from my ex, my friends could have gone running to my ex and told her everything I said. Instead, they allowed me to talk without judging me. I knew I could trust them with my painful emotions, which needed to be shared.

HEALTHY FRIENDSHIPS ARE ABOUT LOYALTY

Being loyal to your friends means you stand by their side regardless of the issues they're facing. We all make mistakes. No-one is perfect. If you screw up, you want to know that your friends have got your back.

HEALTHY FRIENDSHIPS ARE ABOUT RESPECT AND NON-JUDGEMENT

Healthy friends respect your opinions and don't judge you. They make you feel valued and listened to.

How to establish healthy friendships

Healthy friendships actually take a fair bit of work in the beginning. Sometimes it seems like people just become friends automatically, but you need to put time and effort into building a friendship. If you've ever had really close friends though, you'll know the time spent building the relationship is worth it. Personally, I love knowing my best mates are always there for me. They've always got my back.

So, how do you make new, healthy friendships?

BE FRIENDLY

It might sound ridiculous but quite often if you're struggling with making friends, you tend to feel sad. You might also feel angry. If you go around being negative, people won't be attracted to you. (This was me in high school.) Instead, try to be kind, positive and warm towards others. People will naturally respond to kindness because it's something we all want.

FIND COMPATIBILITY

Friendship is about compatibility.

I connected with one of my now closest mates, Steve, 15 years ago because we both wanted to help teenagers going through personal issues. After we got chatting, we learned that we're also both gamers and we both love movies. We didn't find out the commonalities until we spent some time getting to know each other.

Now, we have boys' nights where we go out for burgers and movies. Sometimes, Steve comes over and we'll game and have snacks.

Steve has always been there for me when things went wrong. He was one of the main friends I leaned on when my second marriage broke down.

He'd come over some days and we'd just sit there gaming.

The best thing I like about Steve is that he doesn't need to say anything. He doesn't always feel as though he needs to share advice or 'fix' my problems. It's more that he's *there* for me.

VALUE YOURSELF

We attract people who treat us the same way we treat ourselves. If you value yourself, you'll make friends who respect you. When you feel positive about who you are, it affects how you act as a friend. If you have a healthy self-esteem, you'll be self-confident. This allows you to be real. It means you can be vulnerable.

HAVE FUN IN LIFE

Finally, you should just try to enjoy life and be positive. Have you ever heard the saying 'their smile/laugh was contagious'? It's something everyone is attracted to. Once you stop worrying what people think and start living in the moment, people will naturally be drawn to you. It's an attractive quality.

Remember the last time you laughed so hard tears were streaming down your face and you had a bellyache?

This happened to me when my wife Cherith was pregnant. We had a gender reveal celebration. Our friends made us shoot at a balloon with a nerf gun. Only one of the nerf 'bullets' had a pin in it — and that's the one that popped the

Our pregnancy announcement

balloon and revealed the gender. Cherith and I were so excited to discover we were having a little boy (our baby boy Levi).

Afterwards, my brother-in-law and I had a nerf-gun war (as boys love doing). I accidentally got the bullet with the pin in it stuck in his arm. We were laughing so hard that neither of us could talk. I literally had tears streaming down my face. It was such a good moment.

When was the last time you laughed so hard you were crying? Chances are, it was with a friend.

Managing conflict

Friendships aren't easy. We all have periods where we go in and out of them. There is going to be conflict – healthy friendships involve healthy arguments – but what matters is how you *manage* these.

FIGHT FAIR

When you're having an argument with a friend, make sure you're being fair. Don't deliberately hurt the other person just to get points to win the fight.

DON'T LET NEGATIVITY AND RESENTMENT BUILD UP

If your friend does something to hurt you, say something straight away. If you allow negativity to sit there, unspoken, it will start eroding at your friendship. Instead, make it a priority to work through your issues in a healthy way.

HOW TO HAVE A HEALTHY FIGHT: CHOOSE YOUR RESPONSE

Whenever you have a fight with someone, you *always* have a choice about how to respond:

- *the passive response:* if you're passive, it means you do nothing – this doesn't help.

- *the aggressive response:* when you're aggressive, you lash out or react negatively towards your friend. While you might temporarily feel better, it doesn't solve any problems.

- *the assertive response:* finally, you can choose to be assertive. This involves expressing your point of view, but also listening to your friend's point of view. Both of you need to be able to say, 'When this happened, it made me feel ...'

MASTERING THE ASSERTIVE RESPONSE TO CONFLICT

Assertive conflict is all about open channels of communication. Being assertive means standing up for yourself without aggression. It requires us to know that we have value and not to allow others to mistreat us. In conflict, this means communicating how we feel without aggression.

TALK THINGS THROUGH

Keep talking until you reach a mutual understanding. In an unhealthy friendship, one person is selfish. This person does all the talking and doesn't give the other person an opportunity to express their view. If you're having a fight with your friend, make sure you're giving each other equal opportunity to share your sides of the story.

LISTEN TO EACH OTHER

In a healthy friendship, both people listen to understand. This means paying attention to your friend's point of view and trying to understand where they're coming from. You shouldn't listen just to respond with your own point of view.

DON'T GET OFFENDED

If you get offended easily, you won't be able to take constructive criticism. This is linked to your self-esteem and resilience. If you do get offended, try to let the pain go as quickly as you can.

APOLOGISE

This comes down to being self-aware and having a healthy self-esteem. If you realise you've done something wrong, you need to be able to say 'sorry'. Taking responsibility for mistakes you've made will actually strengthen your friendship and build the respect you have for each other.

LEARN TO FORGIVE

In any fight, you need to be able to forgive – not just your friend, but yourself too. We all have fights; it's normal and it's healthy.

Being able to forgive yourself and your friend after any fight comes down to being self-aware and understanding your thoughts and feelings about a situation. You can consciously choose to let something go. It doesn't necessarily mean you need to forget, but you can choose not to let something affect you anymore.

Your friends won't always be able to respond in a healthy way. They might get defensive, upset or reactive. That's okay. If you're self-aware, you'll realise it's nothing personal. It will be easier to forgive your friend for how they've made you feel.

Being able to forgive isn't just important for your friendships, it's important for your whole life. It's a sign of resilience and something you can choose to work on every day.

Healthy friendships give you natural resilience

When your friendships are healthy, you automatically have people in your inner circle you can turn to for support. Having friends who know you well and care about you means they will call you out on it if you're not acting like yourself. Your friends might help you identify ANTs before you even become aware of them. Friendships don't just enable the human race to survive. A healthy friendship with someone who respects you will help you succeed in life. Healthy friendships take a lot of work; they aren't born overnight. But one thing is for sure: they're worth it!

You've got this!

Answer these questions to revise what you've learned about healthy friendships.

1. Do you think, overall, your friendships are healthy?

   ☐ Yes ☐ No

2. Can you think of any friendships that stand out for you as potentially being unhealthy? Why is this?

   _____

   _____

3. Think about your closest circle of friends. Do these friends fulfil your psychological need to feel like you belong and like you are loved? Why/why not?

   _____

   _____

4. It can be really hard to put yourself out there and make new friends, but healthy friendships are essential for your health and self-esteem. One of the best ways you make new friends is by finding someone with whom you share something in common. For me, I found friends who also like gaming. What are some things about yourself you might share in common with others?

   _____

   _____

5. What sort of friend are you? Do you personally have the qualities of a healthy friend (real and honest, caring and supportive, trustworthy, loyal, respectful and non-judgemental)?

    ☐ Yes – all of them ☐ Yes – some of them ☐ No

    Which quality do you think you need to work on? Why?

    _____

    _____

6. Think about the last time you had a fight or experienced conflict with a friend. Did you respond in a way that was passive, assertive or aggressive?

    ☐ Passive ☐ Assertive ☐ Aggressive

    a. Why do you think you responded this way?

        _____

        _____

    b. If you had a fight/conflict again, would you respond differently? In what way?

        _____

        _____

7. Do you think having healthy friendships affects your self-esteem? In what way?

    _____

    _____

8. After reading this chapter, is there anything about your current friendships you are thinking about changing?

_____

_____

9. What is a goal you can set around making and maintaining healthy friendships?

_____

_____

chapter 8

Real men

This chapter is for the guys out there – but regardless of who you are, there are lessons in here you can learn from.

Growing up, my dad was my role model. I really value my dad. He's hardworking, intelligent and crazy successful in the business world. When I was a kid, I saw him as tough, commanding and strong. He was ex-army, and a big boss at his work. The kids in my street were afraid of him and I looked up to him with a combination of fear and awe. When I'd get upset or hurt myself, Dad would encourage me to 'toughen up' or 'take it like a man'. He also had a saying: 'The irrefutable laws of the universe' (meaning he was always right). For example, he would often say to me, 'It's an irrefutable law that you, Adam, are allergic to pain'. He was usually right, but even if he wasn't right, I always believed him.

Dad had grown up in a time when men didn't talk about their feelings or admit to any weaknesses. He thought he was doing the right thing by teaching me to think the same way.

But things are different these days.

The world has come a long way since my dad was growing up. Now, we know how important it is for all of us, regardless of gender, to talk about our feelings. We need to be self-aware and reach out and talk about our problems. If we don't, it affects our resilience and self-esteem.

What is a 'real man'?

It's hard to know how to act as a 'real man'.

What is a 'real man'? Is it someone who can fight? Lift heavy loads? Someone who's able to 'score' (as in sexual conquests)?

Society is feeding us so many of the wrong messages. What makes – or stops – you from being a real man is about who you are *internally*. It's about your character, integrity and self-esteem. A lot of guys don't know this because they just aren't taught it.

My story

I started talking to teenagers in schools about 'real men' because when I was a teenager, I had no idea what this was. I had the idea in my head that men were supposed to be strong, tough and macho. I felt like I wasn't any of these things.

My school years

During primary school, I never told Dad about the bullying happening at school because I was embarrassed. I didn't want him to think I was weak.

As you may remember from chapter 3, when I reached high school the bullying became so bad, I felt like I couldn't cope. In a moment of desperation, I reached out to Dad and told him what was going on. He told me to 'ignore it' and ended the conversation. His advice was just to ignore everything. As with almost all men from that era, the standard way of dealing with difficult issues was by sweeping them under the rug. So that's what I did. I ignored the bullying. I pushed down the feelings of desperation and despair that threatened to overwhelm me. I don't blame Dad for giving me that advice because he was just teaching me what he knew. But bottling everything up resulted in disaster for me. As it would for anyone.

After Mum and Dad split up, Dad started working really long hours and I hardly ever saw him. When Dad was home, he was distracted. We drifted apart. He stopped being my role model. I felt as though I was drifting aimlessly with no-one to show me the ropes when it came to dealing with life's issues.

Adulthood

In my twenties and thirties, I messed up my relationships and went through two marriage breakdowns because I didn't act like a real man should. I know it sounds like a cop-out, but I didn't know how to act. I thought I needed to shut down emotionally. Be strong and tough. I didn't understand why I was feeling really angry all the time. After my second marriage fell apart, I really struggled with anxiety and depression—an emotional breakdown of sorts. But I got serious about learning from my mistakes and I chose to start focusing on learning how to become a healthy man.

Now I know being a real man is synonymous with being a healthy man. This means being as healthy as you can across all five health gauges (you'll remember we talked about the five health gauges in chapter 5).

You

The more I talk to teenage boys, the more I realise I'm not alone in feeling like I didn't have a male role model who was present and available to me. Having parents who are divorced, or a dad who works FIFO (Fly In Fly Out) or really long hours is pretty normal these days. Even if your dad—or any male you look up to (whether it's an uncle, cousin, stepdad or whoever)—spends loads of time with you, they themselves might feel lost about what it means to act like a man.

How to be a real man

The definition of a real man is personal and different for everyone. I really needed some direction and guidance when I was a teenager about how to even begin, so I hope sharing some advice that I wish I'd received at the time might help you.

Own your issues

As a man, you need to take responsibility for your problems. How often do guys get in trouble and say, 'I didn't do anything, Sir. It wasn't me!'? We all think it's always someone else's fault.

Reality check — it *is* your fault. You need to take responsibility when you do something wrong. If you're struggling with something mentally, you need to talk to someone instead of trying to push your feelings down. Otherwise, those feelings will resurface in other ways. Fear, humiliation, guilt, sadness and embarrassment have a way of morphing into anger and pain until things feel totally out of your control. Have you ever had a rush of rage fill your body? You feel like you're about to explode? Or have you ever suddenly been hit with a deep, dark sadness that feels like a blanket suffocating your body? This happens if you're not *processing* your emotions. (Remember reading chapter 6 on self-awareness and managing emotions?) They're still there, but they're festering. If you don't start talking about your problems, they'll escalate into anger issues, depression and anxiety.

Have self-respect

This means valuing yourself and liking who you are. You need to be self-aware if you want to get to know yourself and what you value. You also need to be open and honest with yourself about whether you're making choices that are good for you.

Respecting yourself means valuing all five health gauges and making decisions to improve your wellbeing. You need to commit to inner growth and self-improvement because you can't respect and value other people unless you respect and value yourself first.

Treat others with respect

We've all heard the saying, 'Treat others as you would like them to treat you'. I think this is such a great way to live our lives in general. It would solve about 890 per cent of our problems! No-one likes being bullied, harassed or talked down to, so let's not treat others that way.

OTHER MEN

The deepest primal need for all men is to feel respected. It's just the way guys are wired.

You probably know you need to feel respected, but you might not always show the same respect to other guys. When you make fun of a mate or fellow student, especially if they are in a position of less power than you, you're attacking their integrity. You're devaluing them and making them feel disrespected. Banter is cool – it's actually healthy in good friendships – but you need to be on equal footing to do it, otherwise it's bullying. Before you rip into another guy, stop for a second and think about how you'd feel if it were you on the receiving end.

WOMEN

Do you treat girls as sex objects or do you show them the same respect as your mates? Guys often think they're entitled to treat girls however they want. They 'perv' on girls and look at them as something that can make them feel good. We don't always do it on purpose, of course. Sometimes I'm watching a movie and I catch myself thinking that an actress is 'hot', but when (if) I think about it, I realise I'm actually being really disrespectful.

You need to treat *all* women with respect. This means that when you're interacting with a girl, she should feel safe, know she is your equal and know you honour and respect her. In the same way, you need to feel respected by the girls you choose to spend your time with.

Care about others

This means you have the capacity to think about others and care about other people. Men are so often portrayed as selfish and only about what they can get.

While that is true of many men, it's not typical. You can't love someone if you don't care about other people. Do you have the capacity to put others first, before yourself or your desires? A real man can. That's the kind of man who makes a great dad and a great husband/partner.

SHOW SELF-CONTROL

For guys, anger comes with feeling like they're not getting treated right. It rises up when they don't feel like they're in control. It's a social emotion that makes you want to punish someone for not treating you the way you want to be treated. Why? Usually, there's pain behind the anger. If you don't use self-control, you tend to lose it. It shrinks like an under-used muscle.

I personally understand how hard it can be to deal with feelings of anger. When I get angry, no matter what I do, I find it really hard to get past it. It's like it consumes me for way longer than it should. I used to be way worse, but it still comes up from time to time. When it does, I have to make a really concerted effort to choose what to do with my anger because there have been a lot of times in my life when it's consumed me, and I've made poor decisions because of it. We'll look at ways to manage anger shortly.

CHOOSE WHAT'S RIGHT

Most people have the capacity to choose between right or wrong. Being a real man means choosing what's right even if you don't feel like doing the right thing. We all realistically know having an affair isn't right, yet so many guys make this decision every single day. They base the decision on how they're feeling and don't practise self-control.

After my last break-up, I was going through a lot of pain and I felt like I was being driven by my emotions instead of my rational brain. I had this strong desire to have a one-night stand. I spoke to my inner circle of friends but only one friend, Ray, gave me a solid answer.

'You care about other people,' he said. 'If you have a one-night stand with a woman, you don't know what she's got going on in her personal life and you might really hurt her.'

That weekend, one of my friends, who's a girl, showed up on my doorstep after a hen's party. She was really drunk (she could hardly walk straight) and she wanted a one-night stand. I could have self-medicated my pain by being with her. The opportunity was landing (pretty much literally) in my lap. But I couldn't do it. I knew, deep down, that it wasn't right.

'Give me your phone, I'm ordering you an Uber,' I said. 'You need to go home.'

It was the right decision because one week later I met Cherith and now she's my wife. I don't know if I would have been in the right headspace to get to know Cherith if I'd taken advantage of my friend's weakness.

###

Two issues directly related to self-control are anger and pornography. These are two issues I struggled with in a huge way when I was a teenager. Let's talk about them, and about why we need to control ourselves.

Getting angry: the three options

| **Suppress** | **Explode** | **Express** |

When you feel angry, you can choose to respond in three different ways:

- *suppress.* This means holding the feelings in and trying not to think about them. It's really dangerous because they build up inside you and turn you into a ticking time bomb. It only takes the smallest thing to make you explode with rage, and then you're out of control.

- *explode.* Another option is to explode. This is when you get really aggressive and let your anger take control. Exploding is also a really dangerous reaction because when you're in this place, you often don't care what you do, to yourself or to others. You need to be able to control your emotions, especially anger.

- *express.* The healthy response to anger is to find out what's triggering you to feel that way and deal with it then and there, using an assertive manner. Follow this process:

  ≈ Recognise how you're feeling.

  ≈ Remove yourself from the situation.

≈ Calm down.

≈ Approach the person who made you feel angry and use an assertive manner to express how you're feeling – but without getting angry all over again.

You can't get aggressive. Being pushy and demanding towards others isn't healthy and it isn't respectful. You can't change how other people act towards you, but you can control how you act in response. It's okay to feel angry, and to *express* that anger, but it has to be to the right person, at the right time and in the right way.

Managing anger issues

If you're feeling angry all the time, there are things you can do to ease how angry you get. Use the following tools to calm your angry thoughts.

CHANGE YOUR THOUGHTS

If you think negatively – *Everything is ruined!* – you'll feel overwhelmed. If you try to think positively about a situation – *This sucks and I'm feeling frustrated, but it's not that bad* – then you'll be able to deal with your anger more effectively.

CHALLENGE ABSOLUTE THINKING

Try not to use absolute terms. For example, you might think to yourself, *This always happens to me* or *I'm never picked for the team.*

I can guarantee it doesn't *always* happen to you, even though it might feel like it.

USE HUMOUR

You can also use humour to diffuse your rage. Personally, I'm not very good at doing this, but I'm aware of it and I'm working on getting better at it. Instead of stewing over your anger and getting more and more wound up, see if you can find a way to laugh at the situation. Then you'll feel like you're in control of your anger instead of your anger controlling you. You just need to make sure you don't fall into using sarcastic humour though because it's unnecessarily mean and hostile. And it's not respectful.

STEP AWAY

Remove yourself from the person, place or issue that's triggering you to feel angry. If your home environment is making you angry, it might mean you need to go and stay with a friend for a few days. You can't not go to school (unfortunately), but you can be self-aware and figure out what's going on at school to make you feel angry and then do something to address it.

FIND TIME TO RELAX

We looked in detail at how to relax in chapter 4. In short, focus on your breathing. Find an activity that relaxes you: head out into nature, have a bath, stream your favourite show on Netflix, do some journaling or read a book.

Dealing with pornography

Why do we need to talk about pornography? Because it's a taboo issue. Even though the age children are being exposed to pornography is getting younger, lots of adults bury their heads in the sand and pretend it's not happening. But pornography is a huge issue. How come?

PORNOGRAPHY RUINS RELATIONSHIPS

Men are wired to enjoy physical attraction. Pornography is designed to appeal to guys. You don't realise it, but watching pornography changes the way you see your partner. Subconsciously, it changes what you expect from them. You start having unrealistic expectations, and it's damaging to the relationship.

I mentioned earlier how pornography engages the reward centre in your brain through the dopamine response. You start needing to watch more to get the same feelings. As a direct response, you start feeling less attracted to your partner. You start feeling isolated. You're more likely to cheat on your partner. And you're more likely to break up.

I made this mistake with my ex-wife. I was struggling for a long time in the relationship. I was in a lot of pain and had no healthy way of dealing with it. After years of feeling stuck in these emotions, I turned to pornography to help me cope. The result? My marriage fell apart.

PORNOGRAPHY PREVENTS HAPPINESS

Watching pornography can make you more likely to experience clinical depression. There's a connection between loneliness and depression. Watching pornography magnifies this. Have you ever heard of erectile dysfunction? For the majority of guys who experience this in their twenties, it's because of pornography use. This would make any man really unhappy!

PORNOGRAPHY LIMITS YOUR SUCCESS IN LIFE

Pornography addiction is real. A third of pornography addicts lose their jobs. Over half of those addicted to pornography experience significant financial loss. Often it's because pornography addiction is linked to a lack of self-control.

PORNOGRAPHY CHANGES YOUR BRAIN

Usually, when people think about pornography, they think about their bodies. Specifically, their sexual organs. Desire, arousal and ecstasy originate in the brain. Earlier in chapter 2, we looked at how neural pathways are created and extinguished. Remember, we talked about the path 'less travelled by' – by choosing to start thinking different, positive thoughts instead of the usual automatic negative thoughts (ANTs). By choosing to think the more positive thoughts, time and time again, you create a new path.

The same neural programming happens in your brain when you watch pornography. When you repeatedly expose yourself to the behaviour shown in pornography, new neural pathways are created. You start seeing what you see on the screen as 'normal'.

PORNOGRAPHY AND THE DOPAMINE RESPONSE

Watching pornography engages all of the four feel-good hormones: norepinephrine, serotonin, oxytocin and dopamine.

The reason pornography is so addictive is because of dopamine. You'll remember we looked at the dopamine response in chapter 5. This is where your brain releases a surge of dopamine in response to pleasure. When you watch pornography and engage in self-pleasure, you get a dopamine release as high as that of a heroin user. If you watch pornography often, you start craving it. You begin needing more of it, and more extreme viewing, to get the same hit of dopamine.

Once you become addicted to pornography, you become trapped in addiction. It becomes something you can't control. It's a destructive cycle where:

- you watch pornography and engage in self-pleasure

- you feel guilty

- you hide what you're doing

- you feel ashamed about what you're doing.

So you turn to pornography to feel better ... and the cycle continues.

Pornography leads to a dark path you don't want to go down. Have you ever heard of convicted serial killer and rapist Ted Bundy? He kidnapped, tortured and raped 27 women. Ted Bundy did an interview with psychologist Dr James Dobson the night before he was executed. Bundy attributes his behaviour to pornography addiction. Every single guy in the same prison convicted of a violent crime started using pornography before committing their crimes. It can escalate out of control and ruin your whole life.

My story

I started masturbating when I was really young. It was early primary school. I discovered it by accident. While other kids my age were running from cooties, I was perving on girls and my teachers. By the time I reached high school, I was struggling big time with bullying and friendships, so I started masturbating to help me feel better.

The first time I discovered pornography was with one of the other kids in my street. We found a magazine and I realised how good it felt to masturbate to the pictures. From there, I started masturbating to anything on TV. Pretty quickly, it was happening up to eight times a day. It felt like an escape for me. When I was watching TV and masturbating, I felt emotionally numb. The dopamine hit that followed made me feel good. At a time when I was feeling stressed out, anxious and depressed about everything going on at home and school, masturbating became my way of coping. In retrospect, I hate that this was my behaviour. I know I can't change the past, but as the man I've now become, I know it wasn't right.

I became really good at perving on girls. I'd sit on the train with my sunglasses on and discreetly look everywhere without anyone noticing. As I mentioned earlier in the book, during high school I got a job at a video shop. Pretty quickly, I realised I could 'borrow' the pornography videos without anyone noticing. I used to stay up all night watching pornography, TV and gaming. Before long, I was addicted. My life spiralled out of control. By the time I reached Year 10, I felt so depressed and anxious that I made a plan to end my life.

Pornography wasn't the only reason I became suicidal, but it played a huge part.

Do you watch pornography? It's normal to think *I won't get addicted.* You feel invincible: *It won't happen to me.* But it will. It can happen to you.

Being a real man is about making healthy decisions

Even if you don't feel like doing something, you might know deep down that it's the right thing to do. Listen to the rational part of your brain instead of being led by your emotions. Use reasoning to consider *What are the consequences of my actions? What will happen if I watch pornography?* And be guided by your conscience: your internal compass of what's right and what's wrong.

To be a healthy man and a real man, you need the capacity to control yourself.

Being a real man is about asking yourself:

- Am I acting with integrity? (Am I being true to myself and living by my values?) Even if no-one is watching me, am I doing the right thing? (Integrity asks you who you are when no-one else is watching.)

- Do I have self-respect? Do I treat girls with respect? Do I treat guys the way I would want to be treated?

- How can I treat others better? Do I care about other people?

- Am I in control of my anger? Do I practise self-control in all areas of my life?

- What can I work on every day to make sure my inner talk and attitude are more positive?

As men, we get to be strong and we get to be tough. But first, we need to think about what these things mean to us:

- Being strong is about having the strength to face our issues and deal with our anger.

- Being tough is about practising self-control and respect.

- Being a real man is about committing to be a 'good guy' who makes the right decisions based on a healthy set of principles.

You have the capacity to be a real man. You've just got to make good choices. It's about being intentional and making the choice.

A great thing happened in a school a few years ago. My team and I had presented to the students 15 times, and one of the topics we spoke about was 'men of respect'. An important part of our approach in schools is talking to teachers about why we discuss particular issues. During one of these sessions, a teacher put her hand up and said, 'I just wanted to share something. This year, my Year 9 boys have changed. They step aside and allow the girls to walk out of the room first. Often, they stay behind and ask if I need help. They've also been pulling each other up and saying, "be a man of respect". This is because of the session you ran, so thank you'.

Why do I share this story? It's not just to blow my own trumpet about Armed For Life (although I am genuinely really proud our presentations are so impactful), it's because the Year 9 boys the teacher was referring to made the choice to be real men. They decided to take the information in the session and act on it. Now, my team members and I tell everyone about their decision! You can make the same decision; the choice lies with you.

You've got this!

Answer these questions to revise what you've learned about being a real man.

1. What does being a 'real man' mean to you, personally?

   _____

   _____

2. Who is a role model for you (who do you look up to)?

   _____

   a. What is it about this person that inspires you?

      _____

      _____

   b. What are the behaviours, personality traits and characteristics of this person that you want to channel?

      _____

      _____

3. Can you think of a man who isn't a 'real man'? Why is this person not a real man?

   _____

   _____

4. If you have a dad who plays a role in your life, how has he affected you when it comes to being a man?

   or

   If you don't have a dad who's present, how do you think this has affected you when it comes to being a man?

   _____

   _____

5. Do you think the media sets a positive image about what a real man is? Why/why not?

_____

_____

_____

_____

6. For me personally, I think being a real man means talking about our issues and owning our struggles. Do you agree?

_____

Is this something that you do, or do you think you need to work on it?

_____

7. What does respect have to do with being a man?

_____

_____

8. How do you manage your anger? Are there ways you could improve how you deal with anger?

_____

_____

_____

_____

chapter 9

Real beauty

When I was in high school, I thought I was ugly. The bullying was so bad I walked around expecting people to make fun of me or laugh at me. Every time I did something dumb, fury would boil inside me and I'd think *I hate myself!*

What does this have to do with real beauty?

At the time, I didn't know the ideas I had about myself were self-fulfilling. My thoughts, actions and beliefs were making me 'ugly'. What does this mean?

'Beauty' is an idea

Beauty is a collection of thoughts you have about something or someone. It's subjective, which means it's in the eye of the beholder. For example, you might have a big, slobbery dog. You might think she's beautiful. Objectively, you know your best friend might not agree. But it doesn't change how you feel.

Who influences how you view beauty?

'Real' beauty is subjective. It's a set of ideas you have about someone or something. There are a few people and factors that can influence how you see beauty. Some of them are:

- your parents or caregivers
- the media
- your friends
- the opposite sex.

Your parents/caregivers carve your ideas about beauty

Your parents (or caregivers) have a huge influence on how you see beauty. In particular, how you perceive beauty in yourself, and how you see yourself. For girls and women, their mums usually play a big role in how they see themselves. If your mum has low self-esteem and places a lot of importance on her looks, chances are you will too.

As I've mentioned before, your home should be a place where you feel loved and like you belong. If you don't get these needs met at home, it can affect how you feel about yourself. But it's not a life sentence. As you know from chapter 1, self-esteem is something you can work on and change.

The influence of the media

Your thoughts about physical beauty aren't always your own. Everyone is influenced by the things around them – for example, advertising or social media.

In general, men don't really understand why girls wear makeup. But whenever I talk to students during Armed For Life sessions, the students who identify as girls/women usually confess they don't leave the house without at least *some* makeup on. Why?

Consider this.

You're probably familiar with the slogan, 'Maybe she's born with it … Maybe it's Maybelline'. One of Maybelline's products is called No Make-Up Makeup. Obviously, it's makeup designed to make you look 'naturally' flawless. It's supposed to give the illusion you're naturally flawless without needing to wear any makeup at all. Um … I see a fatal flaw with this logic. *Obviously*, if you were naturally flawless, you wouldn't need to wear makeup in the first place.

There's so much pressure on women to look flawless and perfect. Think about social media.

I don't know about you personally, but when I talk to students, they usually remark that their feeds are full of 'perfect' people. If it's a professional model/actor/influencer's page, they're getting paid to spend time on their appearance. If it's a business page or amateur influencer, then the images are usually edited, airbrushed and filtered.

You might even download apps to edit your own photos. You might add filters to your selfies. There's nothing *wrong* with this. But think about why you're doing it. Are you changing how you look because you don't like who you really are? Or are you just having fun and playing with your appearance?

You probably know at least one friend (of course it isn't you #wink), who has to check every group photo before it gets posted on socials. This is a red flag for low self-esteem.

How your friends influence the way you see beauty

Your closest friends shape what you think you need to look like. Remember the relationship circles? The people you spend the most time with create who you are. If your friends judge people based on their looks rather than their personality, you'll start noticing appearances too.

It can be difficult not to get caught up in wanting to be friends with someone because they're pretty. Generally, 'pretty friends' equal popularity in high school. It's also a universal idea that popular girls attract 'hot' guys, which equates to high-school success. It's such a flawed concept. Judging yourself and other students based on their looks doesn't bring you connection, personal growth or fulfilment. It doesn't boost any of your health gauges. If anything, it might deplete them.

Guys can influence what you think

As much as we don't want to admit it, most of us worry about what others think of them. The ideas that males tend to have around beauty can influence how you see yourself.

There's a fairly universal belief in Australian high schools that guys like skinny girls with big boobs. This is wrong. There also tends to be the belief that guys value looks over personality. This also isn't true. Perhaps some guys do, but are these the sort of guys you want to be around?

The role of self-image in beauty

The way you see yourself (your self-image) is made up of your inner beliefs about yourself. These beliefs come about because of your thoughts. If you're thinking ANTs all the time, you eventually start believing them. Once a belief becomes ingrained, you start living as though the belief is true – even if it isn't. It's a self-fulfilling cycle that eventually becomes true.

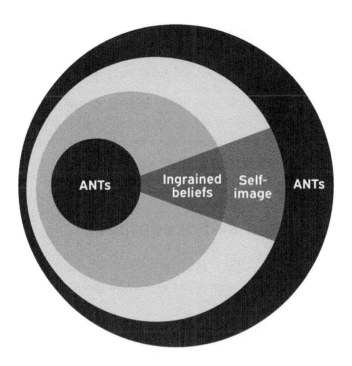

For example, I have scoliosis. It means my spine is curved and as a result, one of my nipples sits slightly higher than the other. I was obsessed with this perceived flaw when I was in high school. I thought everyone was looking at me thinking 'he has wonky breasts'. Obviously, they weren't. (It's not even noticeable.) But because I was so worried about my uneven nipples, it was the first thing my eyes were drawn to when I looked in the mirror. I started holding and carrying myself differently because I didn't want anyone to notice. I thought to myself, *I'm ugly*. I didn't think I had any value (self-worth).

My beliefs about myself affected how I behaved. I didn't command respect from other people because I didn't value myself. It meant I let other students bully me. The students who bullied me found reasons to call me ugly – and I believed them. I fulfilled their ideas about me and my ideas about myself.

So what is real beauty?

If beauty isn't what you look like, then what is it?

Beauty isn't about how you look. However, one thing can be certain: if you respect yourself and have confidence in who you are, you'll behave in ways that boost your health gauges. You'll become resilient, and you'll be at your personal best.

Self-love and self-acceptance

Beauty starts from within. There are plenty of ways to find your inner beauty. Here are some ideas to get you going.

Accept yourself

Being beautiful is about *accepting* yourself. It's also about understanding your identity. Everyone is unique and different. Everyone has different body types and facial features.

Self-love is also about forgiving yourself when you mess up. You develop the capacity to forgive yourself when you really know yourself. Being self-aware gives you the capacity to be compassionate towards yourself and understand why you acted a certain way.

Know your worth

Self-worth is about knowing you have value just as you are.

You don't need to earn acceptance from anyone; not your parents, your friends, your teachers or a guy or girl you like. You're born with value and no-one has the right to make you feel as though you're worthless.

I never knew I had value.

I didn't know I didn't deserve to be treated the way I was being treated by the bullies at school. So, I never stood up for myself.

In a way, I felt like I *deserved* to be bullied at school because I believed I was unlovable. I kept telling myself over and over that I was a loser. That I deserved to get bullied. I came to believe these things. Because I believed them, others did and they treated me exactly the way I 'deserved' to be treated.

Self-worth comes from internal qualities, not how you look or what you're good at. These things can disappear overnight. I know because it happened to me a bunch of times before I developed respect for myself based on my inner qualities.

During high school, I never once thought about what I had to offer. When I think back and reflect, I realise I'm naturally kind and sensitive: I could have helped younger kids who were getting bullied. I'm good at sports: I could have helped with coaching little athletics. I'm not dumb: I could have focused on my schoolwork and been able to contribute a bit more in class.

But instead of focusing on the positives, I was consumed with negative thoughts. I didn't know about my good qualities because I didn't think about them.

Find your internal qualities

Have a think about what qualities you have. What can you offer? If you have low self-esteem, you might automatically think *I have nothing to offer.* This is normal. It's almost impossible to think positively when you're experiencing ANTs and self-limiting beliefs.

One way to discover your innate (internal, natural) qualities is to reflect on your childhood. Who were you before you started worrying about what other people thought of you?

Me

I loved playing chasey and tag when I was little. My brother and I could run full laps around our house, climbing fences and leaping over gates, and I loved the thrill of getting chased or trying to catch my brother or friends. I also had some Master of the Universe toys I loved playing with. I played a lot just by myself because I was naturally pretty quiet, sensitive and introverted.

I really liked playing basketball and going to the movies with Oma and Dad, and I also really liked gaming.

I wanted to become an actor, just because I enjoyed movies so much (and as an immature young boy, I also secretly loved the idea of making out with famous actresses). I've actually got a few actor look-alikes. People tell me I look like Ryan Reynolds, Chris Evans and Aaron Eckhart. Hey, I'm not complaining!

What does this mean?

I've been through some really hard times, but because I'm pretty quiet and sensitive, I'm good at understanding the stuff other people go through. I'm also really good at talking to teens and kids at schools about the stuff I've talked about in this book. It's kind of like acting except it's real stuff, which is arguably more important.

I'm valuable in a team because I bring everyone together. I'm positive and encouraging, and I know that when I go to the movies with people I really care about, it makes me feel closer to them.

All this stuff reinforces my *self-worth*. I know I'm valuable because I have all of these inner qualities to offer. I've had these qualities my whole life, they're just part of who I am.

Try this

It's your turn

Think back to when you were a child.

- What games did you enjoy playing?

- What things did you enjoy doing?

- What did you want to be when you grew up?

Take the time to reflect on these questions and see what you can draw from your answers. Journal some of your thoughts to see what you discover about yourself. Try to think as positively as you can.

Real beauty is priceless

When you start shifting your focus from external looks to your internal qualities, you'll find real beauty. Not only focusing on your internal qualities but learning to accept yourself and love yourself. When you do this, it will become natural to start valuing the way you look and the qualities you actually possess.

Looking in the mirror and liking what you see is something you need to *learn* to do. Focus on being self-aware and thinking positive thoughts about who you are. When the media, friends or guys start influencing how you see yourself, call yourself out on it. Ask yourself, *Why am I getting swayed by fake ideas about beauty?*

Being attentive to yourself and your worth and loving yourself for who you really are is beautiful. When it comes to your resilience, it's priceless. When you give yourself the respect, love and acceptance you truly deserve, you'll be beautiful. When people are in your presence, your positivity will bounce off them like sunlight. You'll have a magnetic sense of capability and your potential will be limitless.

You've got this!

Answer these questions to revise what you've learned about real beauty.

1. What does 'real beauty' mean to you?

   _____

   _____

2. Based on your personal definition, do you think you are beautiful? Why/why not?

   _____

   _____

3. 'When you give yourself the respect, love and acceptance you truly deserve, you'll be beautiful. When people are in your presence, your positivity will bounce off them like sunlight. You'll have a magnetic sense of capability. Your potential will be limitless.' Do you agree with this statement? If so, what inner qualities do you think influence how beautiful you are?

   _____

   _____

   _____

4. Do you think your self-esteem affects your beauty? In what way?

   _____

   _____

5. What does self-worth mean for you? Do you have a healthy sense of self-worth (do you believe you are valuable just the way you are)?

_____

_____

6. How do you think you can use your inner qualities to have an impact on the world around you?

_____

_____

7. What goal can you create around self-worth or self-esteem to improve how beautiful you feel?

_____

_____

8. Think of three women in your life who you consider to be truly beautiful. What is it about them that makes their beauty shine through?

_____

_____

chapter 10

Dating and relationships

Dating and relationships is a subject I'm really passionate about because I know from experience that being in a relationship can be either the most painful thing you go through, or the most rewarding.

The person you are with has a huge impact on who you are and who you become. There's a lot of pressure around being in a relationship or not being in a relationship. Not just when you're a teenager, but when you're an adult too.

The three stages of dating and relationships

The way I see it, there are three distinct stages of relationships:

- the dating stage
- the relationship stage
- the not-currently-dating-or-in-a-relationship stage.

Most of us go in and out of all three stages during our teenage years. One stage isn't better than another; they're just different.

We'll start by looking at the dating stage.

The dating stage

In my opinion, dating is different from being in a relationship. Dating means hanging out and getting to know someone. Being in a relationship implies a certain commitment: that you intend to be with that person for more than just one date.

Being 'attracted' to someone

It can be tempting to go out with someone just because they're 'hot'. While physical attraction plays an important role in ensuring the survival of the human race, it shouldn't be a primary personal consideration.

Our culture places way too much value on being 'hot'. When thinking about dating someone, it's normal to think, *Are they hot? Are they hotter than me?* Think about the last time a friend told you someone was into you. Was your first question, 'Are they hot?' Probably!

If you have a low self-esteem, you might even want to go out with someone who you perceive to be 'hotter' than you because it makes you feel better. This isn't a good reason for jumping into a relationship though.

I made this mistake when I was 19 and I met Natalie.

My story

Natalie was a solid 10/10 on the hotness scale. I was really shallow at the time, and she had all the features I like. When Natalie asked me out, I jumped straight in. We went into full-blown serious relationship mode. Three months later, we were watching fireworks and Natalie broke up with me (who does that, right?). It cut really deep and I was an emotional mess.

A few weeks later, Natalie texted me and said, 'I really miss you. Do you want to go out again?' Of course I did. She was hot, so I jumped straight back in. Full-on relationship mode. Less than 24 hours later, Natalie texted, 'I've made a mistake. I don't want to go out with you'. I was crushed.

A month later, I ran into Natalie and she said to me, 'I'm really missing you. Do you want to go out again?' I said yes. Yep, you guessed right: because she was hot. This time, our relationship lasted a couple of months. One long weekend, we went away with Natalie's parents, her sisters and her sisters' husbands. It sounded like a promising weekend. I thought *What could go wrong?* I didn't even drive my own car. I jumped in with Natalie and her parents. On day one Natalie broke up with me. For the next two days, she messed with me, teasing me with comments such as, 'You want to kiss me, don't you?' It was torture. I thought to myself, *Right, I'm done.*

A month went by, and one night I went out for dinner to Fast Eddy's with some friends. Natalie was in the wider circle of friends, so she came along. I stepped outside to find an ATM and Natalie followed me. She approached me and said, 'You're the only guy for the past six months who hasn't just wanted to be with me for my looks'. I thought to myself, *Umm* (because I actually only wanted to be with her because she was hot). Natalie then said, 'Can we go out again?'

This time I replied with a firm 'No'.

Getting to know someone

The dating stage is really important because it gives you the opportunity to get to know someone before diving in and starting a relationship.

If there's someone you're interested in, the best way to get to know that person is to go to their house. See what they're like in their home environment. (Ask them first; don't just rock up and stare at them through the window. That won't end well.) Look at how they live, and how they treat their family members. Are they kind and caring to their family? When the honeymoon phase of your relationship wears off, they're likely to be kind and caring with you. Are they angry, or aloof? If so, they're likely to become that way with you.

The honeymoon period

When you first start going out with someone, you're usually in the 'honeymoon period'. You've probably heard of this phrase before. It's that brief period where the other person seems 'perfect' (or you don't notice their flaws). Everything this person does is just *awesome*.

The honeymoon phase doesn't last. But some people get addicted to this feeling and mistake it for love. As soon as the honeymoon period is over, they break up with their partner and seek out the same feeling with someone else.

My story

When I was 18, I started dating a girl called Kali. At the time, I was working at a popular pizza joint doing the evening shift (2–10 pm). Kali was my manager. We used to hang out together after our shift. I didn't know Kali already had a boyfriend. One time, about a month after we'd started working together, Kali kissed me. Eighteen-year-old Adam thought, *She's really hot. Relationship ON.* Kali didn't even bother to break up with her boyfriend, and when he found out about me, he was really angry. I didn't care. I was too caught up in Kali.

Two months into our relationship, Kali and I started fighting all the time. One time, we were at a party together. Kali walked off with another guy. Right in front of me, Kali did to me what she'd done with me.

I later found out that Kali had been with multiple partners. She jumped from relationship to relationship. I'm not judging Kali—it's her choice. I'm just saying there's a reason she was behaving this way, and I don't think it was healthy. If I'd taken the time to get to know Kali, instead of just jumping in, I could have avoided all the pain and humiliation.

The relationship stage

I've been through two failed marriages. It's not something I'm proud of. I haven't had many relationships at all. But I had the wrong perception of marriage. It's hard to share this experience, but I know it's something I need to be real and honest about. I feel that if I can help even one person avoid making the same mistakes I did, it's worth sharing my story with you. The overall most important thing I've learned about relationships is to take the time to get to know the person before you jump in.

My story

Both of my failed marriages were unhealthy for two reasons:

- I didn't choose well.

- I hadn't worked on getting myself healthy before jumping into the relationship.

All relationships have baggage. There are always two people, who each bring their own share of experiences and issues. My issues were mostly based around a fear of being abandoned, which stemmed from not having my psychological needs for love and belonging met when I was growing up. When I entered into a relationship, I was always terrified of losing the person I thought I loved.

(continued)

My first marriage barely lasted a year. My second marriage lasted seven years, but it was really damaging on both of us. One really good thing came out of that marriage: my son Cale. He means the world to me, and my ex-wife is an amazing mum to Cale.

After my two marriages, I had one more serious relationship before I met Cherith (my now wife). The relationship seemed perfect on the surface, but we were both struggling with anxiety. I rushed into the relationship without taking the time to reflect and work on myself. As a result, this relationship fell apart as well.

As I mentioned earlier in the book, after this break-up I had an emotional break-down of sorts. I couldn't eat or sleep. My work suffered. I felt more anxious and depressed than I'd ever felt before. I leaned heavily on those in my inner circle during this time. I focused on trying to work on becoming healthier to start feeling better, instead of falling back into old coping mechanisms and addictions.

My turning point: meeting Cherith

I met Cherith at one of the schools I was speaking at, where she was the music and Christian Education teacher, and a form teacher. Cherith was with her form. After the talk, Cherith emailed me. 'Wow, that was amazing. You had their attention the whole time. I just wanted to reach out and offer my encouragement. You're doing an amazing job.'

Cherith and I emailed each other a couple of times before we switched to texting. I could read between the lines and I knew she was keen. I thought to myself, *You should just ask her out*, but I was hurting. I couldn't even think about a relationship.

I was getting a lot of ANTs about how I couldn't cope without my ex. I felt as though I wouldn't survive. I knew I needed to tell myself there were other women out there, it wasn't the end of the world and I would be okay. I thought to myself, *I'll ask Cherith out for a coffee.* It was a way of showing myself I wouldn't actually die without my ex. So, I texted Cherith and asked when she would next be in the city. We organised to have a coffee that Friday at 5.30 pm. Coffee turned into dinner, and dinner turned into drinks. We were out for eight hours in total.

Getting to know each other

I made the conscious decision to be open and honest with Cherith right from the start. I shared my experiences of failed relationships. I confided in Cherith about why I started Armed For Life and the personal struggles I'd experienced growing up. Cherith was open and honest with me too. It felt as though we had so much we wanted to learn about each other. Before we knew it, it was 2 am and I was dropping Cherith at the train station. We decided to catch up again two nights later to go and see a movie.

Once again, the movies turned into dinner and dinner turned into drinks. I felt torn because although I was really enjoying spending time with Cherith, I was struggling with feeling really low and anxious. Cherith asked me, 'Do you want a relationship?' She continued, 'I've been hurt before. I don't want to be hurt again'.

'This is where I'm at,' I explained. 'I've just come out of a nasty break-up. I made a lot of mistakes in my past relationships. I've always jumped in without getting to know the person first. I talk a "big game" to students about how you need to get to know someone before getting into a relationship. I want to do the right thing and start practising what I preach.' Cherith was listening, nodding. I asked, 'Can we hang out, just as friends, for a month and see how things go?'

'Absolutely,' she replied.

For the next month, Cherith and I hung out constantly. There was no physical contact; we didn't even hold hands. We went to the movies, or we just caught up to chat. I was hurting, slowly

(continued)

recovering from my relationship break-up. Cherith was patient, gentle and kind. During this time, I got to know her heart and her character. I was in pain, so I looked past Cherith's looks and got to know the real Cherith. It was just a bonus that she's very attractive—a *massive* bonus. She reminded me of Oma, and this is what drew me towards her. *Okay, this is the right person to start a relationship with,* I decided.

Starting a relationship

Cherith took me out to celebrate my birthday. Towards the end of the night, she said to me, 'Where are we at?' Cherith was meeting some of my friends the next day for a burger, so it was an understandable question.

'I'd really like to be in a relationship together, but I want to go about it the right way,' I said. We chatted for two hours.

I shared with Cherith my fears about falling into another unhealthy relationship. We both had been hurt before and neither of us wanted that again. 'I'm still working on recovering from anxiety and depression,' I revealed. 'I get the anxiety,' Cherith replied. 'I won't give up on you, or quit the relationship because of your anxiety.' This was a big deal for me. We also spoke about co-dependency (I'll explain what this is shortly). We realised we were both the type of people who wanted to spend all our time together. We agreed that we needed to make some firm boundaries around how much time we spent together.

We also spoke honestly about sex, and how we both wanted to wait. For me, even though I'm a Christian, it wasn't a religious decision. It was about self-respect and showing respect towards Cherith. I wanted to start making healthy choices, and for the relationship to be strong and healthy before we were intimate.

Getting married

After a year, Cherith and I got married. Here is a photo of us with my dad and Oma on our wedding day. Cherith and my first son, Cale, have developed a deep bond. Cherith and I have also had a son, Levi, together. Our relationship isn't always easy (sometimes it takes a lot of hard work), but it's the most rewarding thing I've ever been through. I've experienced incredible healing through my relationship with Cherith. She is a gift.

Co-dependence, independence and interdependence

There are three different types of relationship: co-dependent, independent and interdependent.

Co-dependent and independent relationships display an unhealthy attachment in one or both partners. A co-dependent person always needs their partner to be around, whereas an independent person doesn't want their partner to be around.

In our culture, we tend to know that co-dependence isn't a good thing. But sometimes we don't recognise that being independent is unhealthy as well. Someone who is independent in a relationship will draw their value from being on their own and not turning to their partner for support. This can make it difficult to bond with their partner.

The sweet spot in a relationship is *inter*dependence. In my favourite book by Donald Miller (*Scary Close*), the author talks about an exercise on a retreat where partners were instructed to stand on a pillow each. The co-dependent partners put their pillows right up next to each other. The independent partners had their pillows so far away from each other that they couldn't even reach out and touch each other. The interdependent partners had their pillows lined up so they could stand and balance on their own but could reach out for support if they needed it. I think this is the perfect analogy of what an interdependent relationship should be.

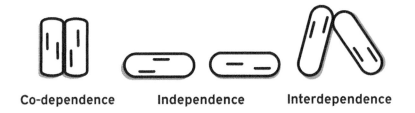

Co-dependence   Independence   Interdependence

Key ingredients for a healthy relationship

From personal experience, I've learned there are four key ingredients to any healthy relationship:

1. You get to be yourself.

2. You set strong boundaries.

3. You learn to love each other.

4. There are certain qualities in the relationship.

In a healthy relationship, you get to be yourself

Too often, people go into a relationship pretending to be someone they're not. They hide things about themselves and pretend to like stuff they don't actually like because they feel it will make them more attractive to the other person. This gets really tiring and it doesn't foster a healthy relationship.

It's really important to be honest about who you are and what you've been through. You don't have to share your entire life story on your first date (although you might — I did!), but you need to have the capacity, once trust has been built, to be honest and real.

A big part of being yourself is being honest about your flaws. It's normal to want to hide the parts of yourself you don't feel comfortable with. But you can't reach the next level of emotional intimacy when you're hiding parts of yourself.

Did you know, the flaws you hide are the ones that grow and thrive?

That's why it's vital to be honest about revealing your flaws to your partner so you can work on them, instead of trying to push them away.

In a healthy relationship, you set strong boundaries

When my son Cale was born, he was huge. He was at the top of the chart for both height and weight. By the time Cale turned six months old, he'd gotten so chunky he was off the chart. He was like a ridiculously cute beached whale.

Cale skipped the crawling stage because he was too big to haul himself around on all fours. Not long after he turned one year old, frustrated at his inability to move, Cale pulled himself to standing and tried running across the room. He'd take a few steps, fall over, pull himself up, take a few more steps and fall. This process continued for a long time. I thought that now Cale was moving, his weight would start normalising, but it didn't. Cale kept getting chunkier. By the time he was 18 months old, Cale weighed 20 kilograms.

One time, I wanted to put Cale in his playpen while I went and had a shower. (I didn't want him roaming around free as I had the oven on.) Cale was a huge Lightning McQueen fan, so I bundled up all the figurines, toys and books and loaded up the playpen. I moved the playpen in front of the TV, put *Cars* on, plonked Cale down and left the room. No sooner had I walked out than Cale ran over to the edge of the playpen, lifted it up with his enormous chunky arms, and climbed underneath in a feat of strongman strength. Cale didn't want to be trapped inside the boundaries of the playpen.

It's human nature to fight against boundaries. We often don't realise the reason we have boundaries is to protect us and keep us safe. A perfect example is the young child of one of my friends, who turned on the tap in the bath when his parents weren't looking. The water scalded him, and he ended up with burns all over his body.

While we're talking about physical safety in the examples above, boundaries also play a role in keeping you psychologically safe and mentally healthy. Sometimes you might have boundaries set in place for you (for example, your parents might set boundaries around what time you need to be home at night, or how long you can spend gaming). Other times, you need to take it upon yourself to set some boundaries.

When it comes to relationships, you need to set strong boundaries around time, physical touch, and sex and intimacy.

BOUNDARIES AROUND TIME

It's not healthy to spend every minute of every day with anyone. I know how tempting it is to want to spend all your time with someone when you're crazy about them. It's something I struggle with myself. The key is to make time for your own hobbies or social activities.

If you feel as though you need to be with your partner all the time, you'll start becoming a needy person. It's not an attractive quality.

Cherith and I had a natural boundary when we started dating as she lived in Mandurah, which is an hour away from where I lived in Perth.

BOUNDARIES AROUND PHYSICAL TOUCH

Some couples need to be touching each other all the time. They can't even eat a burger without touching. I'm an affectionate person and I'm into physical touch, but I recognise it's okay to not need to be touched every single second – especially when I'm eating a burger.

Anyone who knows me well knows I love my burgers. (I even have a 'Top 5' list of burgers in Perth!)

BOUNDARIES AROUND SEX AND INTIMACY

Having boundaries about how far you're willing to go sexually is absolutely essential for emotional health. Going 'too far' sexually is really risky. When you have sex with someone, you give away a part of yourself. If you sleep with too many people, you'll have nothing left of yourself to give.

Aside from the emotional risks, pregnancy and STIs are real. It's not one of those things that 'won't happen to me', even with contraception.

RESPECTING EXTERNAL BOUNDARIES

As a teenager, it's normal to want to rebel against the boundaries your parents or caregivers put in place for you. However, even if you don't agree with the boundaries put in place, learning to stick to these boundaries allows you to establish self-control. When you start pushing back on boundaries and rebelling, you tend to start lacking self-control. It's a pattern of self-destruction that can last for the rest of your life.

In a healthy relationship, you learn to love each other

A healthy relationship involves two people who love and care about each other. There needs to be a mutual capacity to love each other.

Some people struggle with loving another person. Does the person you're with actively listen when you talk? Or do they just want to jump in and talk themselves? Is your partner able to stand back and focus on you, or is everything about them? You don't want to be in a relationship with someone who's selfish. I've been there. Regardless of how 'hot' the person is, they become unattractive really quickly when the relationship is all about them.

A book I love, and highly recommend, is *The Five Love Languages* by Dr Gary Chapman. Chapman speaks about how every person has their own 'love tank' (a bit like a petrol tank) that needs to be kept topped up. This doesn't just apply to romantic relationships; children need their tanks filled with love from their caregivers too.

There are five different types of fuel that can be used to fill your love tank (these are Chapman's 'love languages') and everyone needs a different type of fuel.

For example, your love language might be 'acts of service'. Your love tank is topped up a bit when your partner makes you a cup of coffee, cooks dinner or cleans the house (or your caregiver does your maths homework for you – I'm totally not endorsing that by the way).

Your partner's love language might be 'physical touch' – an unexpected hug will do the trick. But if you try to show this person how much you love them by making them dinner or saying 'you're beautiful', it won't top up their tank. This is because you're not speaking their 'love language'.

There are certain qualities in a healthy relationship

Healthy relationships comprise two people with the following qualities.

- They both have personal responsibility and can own up to their mistakes. If they both have this quality, it gives them the ability to work on anything. That's why this is the number-one quality on the list.

- They trust each other. Trust is essential: no matter what, you can't have a healthy relationship without trust. If you don't trust your partner and you're constantly wondering what they are doing on their phone, you have a problem – and vice versa. It goes both ways.

- No matter what, they think the best of the person they're with and trust they will do the best thing by them.

- They respect each other and understand they're different people with different families and different upbringings, and they don't try to change each other. Respect means value: we have to trust that our partner values us, which can be hard if we're struggling with other issues or if we've been hurt by our partner. We have to choose to be respectful of each other, regardless of what's going on in our relationship.

- They can sacrifice and compromise. It means they can both give up a little for each other at times.

- They can both forgive each other and ask for forgiveness. When we hold on to unforgiveness it breeds resentment and bitterness, which leads to contempt.

- They're committed, meaning they're with that person no matter what and know the other person feels the same way towards them.

The not-currently-dating-or-in-a-relationship stage

It's normal to go in and out of relationships, especially during your teenage years so let's focus on 'if you're not in a relationship' here. When you're not in a relationship, there are still thoughts and actions you can focus on so that when you do go into a new relationship, you're in a strong and healthy position. So, what should you focus on when you're not currently in a relationship? You should focus on:

- not needing to be in a relationship

- finding out what you want

- working on yourself.

Not needing to be in a relationship

Wanting to be in a relationship is fine, but as soon as you feel as though you need to be in a relationship, you become needy. This was me. For the entire five years of high school, I went from crush to crush to crush, never asking any girls out because I thought they wouldn't like me. I was scared I'd be rejected, so what was the point in asking?

After school, I went from relationship to relationship, without a break. I *needed* to be with someone all the time and I was never happy on my own. We spoke about co-dependence, independence and interdependence earlier. If you become co-dependent (meaning two people in a relationship *need* to be together instead of *wanting* to be together) then the relationship is doomed.

Of course, being totally independent — that is, not letting yourself lean on your partner for anything — also destroys relationships. It's like a badge people wear that can ruin future relationships.

It's only in interdependency that relationships can flourish with two healthy people. They can lean on each other, stand on their own and do their own thing, and achieve amazing things together.

Finding out what you want

Take the opportunity to get to know what you want in a partner. Or, get to know what you don't want. What are the red flags? What are your absolute no-go zones? Everyone is different, and what *you* want in a relationship will be different from what your besties want. Your red flags will be different from your friends'. For example, you might not be able to stand it if someone can't mind their temper, is addicted to porn or wears too much makeup.

When I got to know Cherith, I thought she might be amazing because she didn't have any of my red flags (and it turns out she *is* amazing). Get to know yourself and what you want. You don't have to have a 40-point checklist; just know your deal breakers.

Working on yourself

Use practices around self-awareness to ask yourself, *What would it be like to be in a relationship with me?* Have a look at the components of a healthy relationship and assess whether you have these qualities:

- Am I honest?

- Do I wear a mask?

- Am I selfish?

- Can I set boundaries?

- Do I have self-control?

- Can I trust people?

- Can I take responsibility for the things I do wrong?

- Am I respectful?

The reason why working on yourself and your own personal growth is important is that when you go into a relationship, you want to take the best version of yourself into it.

Relationships and the five health gauges

Relationships (relating) are involved in one of the five gauges of health and wellbeing that I introduced you to in chapter 5, namely the relational gauge. Your social connections are really powerful because humans are designed to live in connection with each other. If you're in a toxic relationship, all of your health gauges are affected and it's difficult for you to function at your best. You might be triggered and slip back into addictions without realising it. This happened to me. Everything falls apart during a toxic relationship and you lose yourself. If you're in a relationship and something happens that triggers you to feel awful, you need self-awareness to identify what has upset you and recognise your emotions so you can be healthier in the relationship.

Your relationships are also linked to your self-esteem.

When you have low self-esteem, you tend to choose really poor relationships. You might allow people to treat you in a really poor way because you don't think you're worth anything. And you might not think you deserve any better. When you lack resilience and you run into problems in your relationship (every relationship has problems) you'll fall apart and you won't be able to resolve the issues. If you lack resilience, you're guaranteed to have a toxic relationship.

To set yourself up for a healthy relationship you need to be confident in yourself and on your own. If you can take the time and opportunity to work on yourself and get yourself to the best place you can possibly be, when you do meet someone who fits what you want in a partner, your relationship will be healthy. Relationships can be the most rewarding thing in life if you make the right choices and develop honesty, trust and interdependence.

You've got this!

Answer these questions to revise what you've learned about dating and relationships.

1. Do you think there's a difference between dating and being in a relationship? What's the difference?

   _____

   _____

2. Are you in a relationship? Do you think it's a healthy relationship? Why/why not?

   _____

   _____

3. If you're in a relationship, do you get to be yourself or do you feel like you have to wear a mask? Why is this?

   _____

   _____

4. If you're in a relationship, do you think you and your partner both have a healthy self-esteem? Do you feel confident with the boundaries you've set in your relationship?

   _____

   _____

5. If you're in a relationship, do you feel confident you're capable of loving the person you're with?

   _____

6. If you're in a relationship, do you feel like both you and your partner have a healthy sense of self-esteem, resilience and the ability to manage stress?

_____

What is something you think each of you could work on when it comes to your inner resources?

_____

_____

7. If you're single, are you happy being single? Why/why not?

_____

_____

8. What sort of qualities would you want in a partner? What is important to you? And what are the no-go zones?

_____

_____

9. What would it be like to be in a relationship with yourself? Would you like the person you were dating?

_____

_____

10. If you've ever been in an unhealthy relationship, did it affect your self-esteem? In what way?

_____

_____

Do you think you've recovered from this relationship? If not, what steps can you take to move forward?

_____

_____

chapter 11

Drugs, alcohol and other addictions

Do you know what you want in life?

Most of us want to become great at the stuff we love and enjoy. We want to like ourselves and feel good about our accomplishments. We want to feel like we are loved, respected and admired.

Is what you are doing right now taking you away from the life you want to lead? The choices you make about what you do and who you hang out with don't just affect you right now. They'll influence who you become tomorrow.

Making healthy decisions about drugs and alcohol

If you're unsure about whether or not you should do something, think to yourself, *Are there more positives or are there more negatives?* Not just now, but in the future.

Think about the next party or social gathering you're headed to. Will there be alcohol there? Are you planning to drink? Instead of thinking, *everyone is drinking* and following the crowd, take a moment to think about what the alcohol will actually do to you.

Decisions about drinking alcohol

Alcohol is a depressant drug that slows down messages travelling between the brain and the body. It's a poison. When you drink it, your body freaks out and tries to get rid of it as quickly as possible.

HOW ALCOHOL AFFECTS YOUR BRAIN

When you down a Cruiser (or whatever your usual alcoholic drink of choice is), the alcohol works its way into your bloodstream and into your brain. While the depressive effects of alcohol are well known, you might not realise the stimulative effects it can have.

Neurotransmitters are the brain's chemical messengers. Alcohol jacks up one of the inhibitory neurotransmitters in your brain called GABA. The role of GABA is usually to decrease certain brain signals and activity in your nervous system. It's why you get that feeling of relaxation after a drink. The more you drink, the more the activity of the GABA receptors are increased. That's why, after too many drinks, people start stumbling and acting clumsy.

Drinking too much alcohol can overstimulate your GABA pathways. This causes extreme sedation of the central nervous system (this is what happens when someone is totally 'paralytic'). It leads to alcohol toxicity and overdose.

Over time, desensitisation of your GABA receptors can start making you feel stressed and anxious. You'll feel triggered to drink more alcohol to get those same relaxed vibes. Pretty quickly, your tolerance skyrockets. Alcohol becomes a coping mechanism and derails you into addiction.

Alcohol also triggers the dopamine response. Remember, this is what happens when your brain senses you're doing something pleasurable. By jacking up the reward centre in your brain, alcohol tricks you into thinking you're doing something pleasurable (even though you're literally downing a poison).

If you're feeling low, chances are, drinking alcohol will temporarily make you feel better. But at the same time, you're altering other brain chemicals that enhance feelings of depression.

ALCOHOL IS A COPING MECHANISM

If you're feeling stressed, anxious or depressed, it's normal to automatically turn towards the things you know will make you feel better. While alcohol makes you feel more relaxed/less anxious, more social/less self-conscious, more exciting/less boring, it also magnifies your feelings at the time. If you're already feeling angry, you'll start feeling angrier. If you're already feeling depressed, alcohol will make you feel even more depressed.

The trouble is, while alcohol might sometimes make you feel better temporarily, it makes you feel so much worse about yourself – even the next day.

If you drank too much and you ended up drunk, you would have started thinking you were more fun to be around than you actually were. You wouldn't have realised you were slurring, falling over, getting aggressive and saying stupid things. You might have become dependent on your friends to look after you (which gets tiresome for them pretty quickly), and you might have thanked them by punching them in the face or spewing on them.

You know the feeling of *I'm never drinking again*? You might be feeling regret about some of the stuff you did or said the night before, or you might not even remember.

Chances are, you drank too much alcohol because you were using it as a coping mechanism.

HOW ALCOHOL AFFECTS YOUR BODY

Even one alcoholic drink can affect the quality of your sleep, and how good you'll feel the next day. One Finnish study found that even one drink can diminish your sleep quality by 9.3 per cent, while getting drunk can reduce your sleep quality by up to 40 per cent. Can you afford to lose a night of good sleep? How will this affect your stress levels, thinking and performance? Will it affect your ability to achieve your goals?

Alcohol also messes with your blood sugar. It raises the cortisol in your body, making you feel stressed out and increasing your inflammation. If you drink regularly, you'll gain weight, get acne, start feeling sick to your stomach and have a messed-up digestive system. You'll start feeling stressed, sick and tired all the time and you'll constantly be trying to fight off colds and infections. Drinking also affects your fitness. If you go to the gym or play sports, even one night of drinking affects your ability to perform at your best.

Weed and other drugs

What about smoking weed?

It's harmless, right?

Unfortunately, it's not. Think about what you want in life. Then think about whether weed is going to take it away from you.

Weed stops your brain from functioning properly. You get stuck on one thought. Automatic thinking is negative – it's just human nature – so you end up stuck on one negative, repetitive thought. Weed isn't nicknamed 'dope' for no reason.

Weed makes you anxious–sometimes straight away. I have spoken to a number of students in my one-on-one counselling that have smoked weed ONCE and couldn't leave the house. Thankfully after working together that changed. Maybe not immediately, but eventually the dopamine response will become dulled and you'll start needing more and more to get the same effect. Weed will become your coping mechanism, and you'll start feeling anxious and depressed without it. Eventually, you might develop paranoia or even schizophrenia.

Like other mind-altering substances, weed also affects your ability to learn and grow. It holds you back in all areas of your life. You might think weed is harmless, and just a bit of fun with friends. But every time you choose to smoke weed, you're choosing to hold yourself back.

TAKING DRUGS

I doubt many primary school kids write 'heroin user' when they're asked what they want to be when they grow up. I doubt they write 'drug dealer' either. My son Cale is eight and he says he wants to be an archaeologist, but he doesn't actually know what that means.

Whatever substance you choose to take (even if it's just an entry-level drug or something you see as harmless) loses its effect after a while. You'll end up chasing the dopamine hit and eventually you'll move on to something stronger. Even if you think you won't, it's inevitable. That's how addiction works. If you ask anyone who's addicted to heroin why they started taking it, they'll usually tell you they were addicted to a different drug first.

If you're feeling like you want to try drugs, it's a warning sign in itself. Why do you want to take drugs? Why do you feel like you need to do something destructive to make yourself feel better? It's important to practise some self-awareness and think things through.

My story

When I was a teenager, I didn't choose drugs and alcohol because they never really came up for me. That's not to say I wouldn't have turned to drugs and alcohol if the opportunity had arisen—I was in so much pain that I probably would have. I was getting bullied and I was outcast. I was also insecure and shy, so I was never invited to social situations where there was a lot of drinking or drug taking.

(continued)

This all changed when I turned 17. I started partying too hard, and I didn't respect myself because I had low self-esteem and low self-worth. I went through a period of a year or so when I turned towards drinking and partying, and I slept with different girls during this time because I thought that was what I was 'supposed' to do. Now I look back and I wish I hadn't treated myself and other people the way I did. But I know I can't change the past, so I'm focused on writing myself a better future.

During high school, my coping mechanisms were binging on junk food, gaming addiction and pornography addiction. I understand how you think what you're using is helping you. It's making you feel better; it's numbing your pain. Why would you want to change? It can be so hard to see past the immediate relief you get from a coping mechanism when you're feeling really stressed, anxious or depressed.

I was in this place myself. I didn't want to stop gaming, or watching pornography, even when I knew it was making everything worse. My coping mechanisms were the only thing that gave me an escape. It wasn't just a physical escape either. My coping mechanisms gave me an emotional escape from the anxiety, depression and sense of despair that was taking over. I didn't realise it was a self-perpetuating cycle, which was actually making the anxiety, depression and despair worse.

How poor decision making affects your brain

You can think of the neural pathways in your brain as 'freeways' and 'highways'. When you make a decision, you're activating different neural pathways (or roads) in your brain.

Think about a roadmap of your local city (for me, it's Perth in Western Australia). There are both freeways and highways.

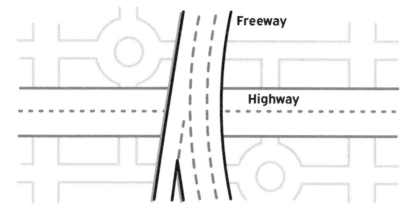

Freeways are the biggest roads. Highways are still a lot bigger than normal roads, but they aren't as significant as freeways.

When you're using something as a coping mechanism, it's like a highway (or a freeway in construction). If you stop using the coping mechanism, the highway will shrink back down to a road. If you continue to use a coping mechanism and it becomes a major freeway it'll be there for the rest of your life. You'll quickly become trapped in the cycle of addiction.

Focus on your goals

If you focus on developing a strong mind – if you know what you want in life and who you want to become – then you'll be less distracted by stuff that makes you feel good in the short term. You'll know it's not worth it in the long term. You'll be motivated by your bigger goals, and you won't want to sacrifice them just to feel good. If you're struggling with low self-esteem, or if you're feeling really stressed out and hating yourself, it's easy to turn to things that aren't good for you because you're desperate to feel better.

Breaking free from drugs, alcohol and other addictions

The steps to break free from drugs, alcohol and other addictions are:

1. Acknowledge the problem.

2. Avoid your triggers.

3. Stay accountable to yourself and others.

Acknowledge the problem

If you can look at yourself honestly and accept you've got a problem, then you've already taken a huge step. You need to acknowledge something isn't right *before* you can make any changes.

Avoid your triggers

It's important to be purposeful about any situations that will tempt you to use. If you're in a bad place mentally and you're finding yourself leaning on drugs or alcohol to cope, you need to choose not to go to a party where you know there's going to be drinking and drug use.

If you have a good friend, ask them if you can do something else to distract you from the party. In moments of pain, distraction becomes your best friend. If you don't have a good friend, turn back to chapter 7 ('Healthy friendships') and focus on finding some. It's really important to have friends who help you make positive choices and support you when you're going through a difficult time. Lean on your inner circle as much as you can.

Sometimes, you might need to break free from your current friends if you want to break free from drugs and alcohol. It's a strong, positive choice in the right direction, and the people in your life who are healthy and want the best for you will respect you for your decision.

Stay accountable to yourself and others

Thirdly, you need to stay accountable. Tell someone what's going on. Reach out and ask for help. It's important to talk to a trusted adult. Not because you want to get into trouble, but because a trusted adult can support you and hold you accountable for your actions.

It's almost impossible to recover from an addiction on your own. You need to be open and honest with yourself and others instead of trying to hide your actions. Anything you keep in darkness or secrecy tends to grow and thrive. And don't lie about it: if you want to get healthy, you need to be real. Even when you stuff up.

You might want to reach out and talk to your friends about what's going on for you, and that's okay too, but they can't be the only ones you talk to if you want to succeed. Someone who is a trusted adult has been through stuff in their lives too, and they know how to support you. You can reach out and talk to your school psychologist or counsellor, chaplain, or if you're not sure where to go, start with a teacher you like and trust.

Practising the skills you've learned

Drugs are something you lean on when you're struggling or experiencing pain. If you're feeling vulnerable or like you might give in to peer pressure to take drugs or drink, it's important to make use of the tools you've learned so far in this book:

- *Be self-aware:* pay attention to how you're feeling and what's making you feel this way. How are you thinking? Are your thoughts negative? If so, challenge them. Reframe a repetitive thought into a positive one.

- *Actively work on improving your self-esteem:* choose healthy friendships and relationships, live a healthy lifestyle and reach out and talk to someone.

- *Work on becoming more resilient:* work on understanding yourself and identifying what's triggering you to feel bad about yourself.

- *Address any mental health issues you're experiencing.*

- *Reach out and ask for help*: if you're getting bullied or if you've got stuff going on at school or at home, talk to a trusted adult.

Owning your issues to be resilient

We all go through stuff in life; we all have problems. You need to own your issues and commit to dealing with the stuff that's holding you back. Self-medicating problems with coping mechanisms such as drugs or alcohol will never work. Life is about experiencing personal growth and meaningfulness. The way to achieve this is through trying to be as healthy as possible across all five health gauges.

To do this, you need to overcome your fear of letting go of your coping mechanisms and make a decision that, *Today, you will change. Today, you will choose to do what moves you towards what you want in life.*

You've got this!

Answer these questions to revise what you've learned about drugs and alcohol.

1. What do you think of when you hear the terms 'druggie' or 'alcoholic'?

   _____

   _____

2. Have you ever felt pressured to take drugs or drink alcohol? How did you respond? If the same situation occurred again, do you think you would respond in the same way?

   _____

   _____

3. Have you had, or do you know someone who's had, a problem with drug or alcohol addiction? How did it affect you/them?

   _____

   _____

   _____

   _____

4. Do you think working on your own self-esteem will alter how you think about drugs and alcohol?

   _____

   _____

5. Do you think people who drink alcohol or take drugs can be physically and psychologically healthy? Why or why not?

_____

_____

6. How would taking drugs or drinking alcohol affect your own life, both immediately and in the long term?

_____

_____

7. Do you think relationships and friendships where drugs and alcohol are involved are healthy friendships/ relationships? Reflecting on your own relationships and friendships, how would drugs/alcohol affect them?

_____

_____

8. When it comes to drugs and alcohol, do you feel like you do 'what is right'? How could you be truer to yourself?

_____

_____

Conclusion

Are you ready to take the road to resilience?

The point of this book is to show you that you can choose to become the best version of yourself right now – you don't have to wait until you're older, or smarter, or richer, or more ripped, or hotter ... or whatever.

Starting to make changes, being resilient and choosing to feel good about yourself starts you out on the road to resilience. Being self-aware, having good friends and relationships and being healthy in all five health gauges means you will move forward in life. Choose to take control of your life instead of letting your life and emotions control you.

I started Armed For Life because of my own experiences as a kid and growing up.

I hope this book has helped you to feel more confident and ready to deal with life and growing up, or, if you're a parent or teacher, it's helped you to understand the issues we all go through and how to help someone who's struggling.

It's important to me to be honest and real about what I've been through because when we know someone else understands how we're feeling or why we're doing the stuff we're doing, it's easier to reach out and ask for help.

At Armed For Life we run sessions and workshops in schools, provide one-on-one counselling and run bi-annual camps – and we have a bunch of online resources for you to access too. We've also got an online program you can take part in. You can find more information on our website at www.armedforlife.com.au or visit us on our socials: @armedforlife and #armedforlife.

Where I'm at, personally

I've come a long way from the Adam I was in high school. Instead of waking up each morning feeling sick to my stomach with dread, I wake up feeling grateful. The morning light streams through my window and I'm drawn towards it, instead of wanting to dive back underneath the covers. When I think about the day ahead – even if it's going to be really busy and stressful – I make sure I've got enough time to recover and fine-tune my gauges and refuel my love tank because I know these are really important if I want to keep moving forward and living my best life possible.

I know it sounds cheesy for me to say, 'My life is great, everything's good' but it really is. I feel better than I've ever felt before and I'm thankful for everything I have. I love my work, the organisation I've created and the people in it.

My faith is central to my life. I know I'm not perfect. I'm very aware of my faults and flaws (probably more aware than I've ever been before), but I don't focus on them. I can recognise the things I'm not good at, and the things I struggle with, and it's a constant journey of trying to work on these things. I still get negative thoughts – that's normal; we all do – but I get heaps less than I did before. My self-esteem is healthy, and this means a lot to me because I struggled so much as a kid and as a teenager.

I know I've got things to work on. I'm busy and I can get overwhelmed at times because I'm trying to grow my business and I want to help as many people as I possibly can. But I can manage my external stressors better because I've got my internal stress levels under control (most of the time, anyway). When personal problems come along, I sometimes struggle with bouncing back afterwards. But I've learned that expressing my emotions is really important and I'm getting good at managing problems that come up.

My mental health is definitely far better than it's ever been before. Anxiety is really rare. When it does come up, I know how to manage it.

It feels like a long time ago that I was stuck in a cycle of addiction and self-destruction, but at the same time I know how important it is to be aware of the things that trigger me to fall back on old coping mechanisms.

Physically, I think my body is healthier than it's ever been before. It's pretty cool being in my forties and being the healthiest I've ever been. I make good choices with food; I'm heading back to playing basketball with no ACL, after tearing it a second time; and I'm even gaining a bit of muscle in the gym.

It's funny how, right up until my thirties, I didn't feel like a man at all, even with all the things I'd been through and experienced. There's still an element of that and I'm going to continue to explore it, but at the same time, I actively try to be a healthy man by taking responsibility for my issues, respecting myself and others, showing self-control, caring about others and making good choices.

In terms of the people I surround myself with, I've got really good, quality friendships, and I'm grateful for that every day. My 'inner circle' mean a lot to me because they supported me through my darkest times and now I have the opportunity to support them. I question every now and again whether I'm a good friend or not because I guess I'm really still learning about friendships.

With Cherith, Cale and our puppy, Parker, in our new house

Sometimes I think, *I always have to initiate stuff. Does that mean they don't want to hang out with me? What's wrong with me?* and I have to catch myself doing it, and challenge those thoughts.

I am absolutely in love with my sons and my wife, Cherith. I adore them and I love that Cherith loves me (warts and all). Our relationship brings out the best in both of us, and my heart swells when I think about what the future holds.

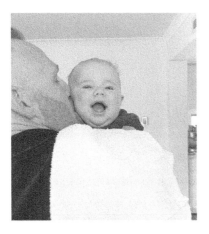

My second son, Levi

When my Oma passed away I was left wondering where she is now. Is she really in heaven? It shook my faith a bit, but I worked through it and prayed a lot. When I stop and think about her, I still get teary, but that's okay. Oma taught me what it means to care about other people. She was always there for me when I needed her, even when she wasn't aware of it. She loved me, even when I couldn't love myself.

She believed in me, no matter what. When I was at my lowest point, in Year 10, and I was ready to take my own life, it was only the thought of my oma that stopped me.

Things are great with Dad these days. He's softened up a lot in the past few years. Whenever we catch up, he always says to me, 'Son, you always make me think about myself and it's always challenging. But in a good way'. I love him a lot and I'm really thankful for the things I got from him.

I love my mum too and our relationship is going really well. It's a slow-growth journey I'm trying to continue purposefully. We had a beautiful moment recently where we sat down together and I asked her to be more involved with Cale and Levi. Mum said yes, which made me happy.

The future of Armed For Life

I know I'm on a continual path of growth, but I love who I am. I love where I am and I know I'm going to continue to grow, work on my flaws and celebrate my wins, whether they're personal wins in my own journey, or a win for Armed For Life and something we achieve. I want to keep succeeding with Armed For Life and extend our reach so we can touch the lives of as many people as possible. Up to this point, we've spoken in more than 500 schools to more than one million students. We play an important role in visiting workplaces all over Western Australia, talking to staff about resilience, self-esteem and self-development. We're working a lot with city councils, especially in their primary-school-to-high-school transition programs. And I'm excited to announce that Armed For Life will be opening branches in other states of Australia and around the world.

Our charity, the Armed For Life Foundation, has recently been approved, which means we can start taking donations and applying for grants to run our sessions in schools that otherwise couldn't afford it. Last year, Armed For Life travelled to South Africa where we've started a

Armed For Life's first international trip to South Africa

Presenting to students on resilience in South Africa

really productive partnership with Jarryd Smith at 2nd Chance. We've also started the Global Change Agency, so stay tuned for exciting new developments.

Personally, I believe in God and I know He has plans for me, and I'm going to go with them, whatever those plans may hold. I'm just excited, and I haven't been this excited before, so it's a pretty wonderful place to be. Life is great. I'm going to continue to learn, continue to work on things.

If I could have given myself a picture of this in my teenage years – to see all the things I've accomplished – it would have changed my perception back then.

This is what I want for you: to see that there is hope.

There is possibility.

And that we all have unlimited potential to become the very best version of ourselves, whatever that may be.

Choose the road to resilience.

Be armed for life.

Adam Przytula
Director, Armed For Life

Index

Printed and bound by CPI Group (UK) Ltd, Croydon, CR0 4YY

17/01/2022

03104167-0001